Building Your eBay Traffic the Smart Way

Other Books by Joseph T. Sinclair

eBay the Smart Way
eBay Business the Smart Way
eBay Motors the Smart Way
eBay Global the Smart Way
eBay Photography the Smart Way

Building Your eBay Traffic the Smart Way

Use Froogle, Datafeeds, Cross-Selling, Advanced Listing Strategies, and More to Boost Your Sales on the Web's #1 Auction Site

Joseph T. Sinclair

AMACOM

American Management Association
New York • Atlanta • Brussels • Chicago • Mexico City • San Francisco
Shanghai • Tokyo • Toronto • Washington, D.C.

Special discounts on bulk quantities of AMACOM books are available to corporations, professional associations, and other organizations. For details, contact Special Sales Department, AMACOM, a division of American Management Association, 1601 Broadway, New York, NY 10019.
Tel.: 212-903-8316. Fax: 212-903-8083.
Web site: www.amacombooks.org

This publication is designed to provide accurate and authoritative information in regard to the subject matter covered. It is sold with the understanding that the publisher is not engaged in rendering legal, accounting, or other professional service. If legal advice or other expert assistance is required, the services of a competent professional person should be sought.

Library of Congress Cataloging-in-Publication Data

Sinclair, Joseph T.
    Building your eBay traffic the smart way : use froogle, datafeeds, cross-selling, advanced listing strategies, and more to boost your sales on the web's #1 auction site / Joseph T. Sinclair.
        p. cm.
    Includes bibliographical references and index.
    ISBN 0-8144-7269-9
    1. eBay (Firm) 2. Internet auctions. I. Title.
HF5478.S473 2004
658.8'7--dc22   2004024907
                                                              CIP

Printing number
10 9 8 7 6 5 4 3 2 1

To my extraordinarily talented friends and colleagues, who were members of the North Bay Multimedia Association of the San Francisco Bay Area, including Lee Callister, Mike Campos, Steve Kirk, Ann Smulka, Michael Wanger, Joe Zizzi, Sharon Rockey, Steven Gilman, Sherry Miller, Ken Milburn, Bob Dougerty, Ross Millerick, Janine Warner, Jeff Schriebman, Bruce Ford, Luong Tam, Roy Nolan, Arleta Quesada, Ron Pellegrino, Terry McNally, Bruce Ford, Melinda Bell, Don Means, and Bob Charlton

Contents

Acknowledgments

As I am finishing this book in October 2004, it is the tenth anniversary of my first website. It was the Fine Food Emporium, the first gourmet food store on the Web. I would never have done it without being a member of the North Bay Multimedia Association (NBMA) of the San Francisco Bay Area, a group of talented professionals from various media. Lee Callister showed us Mosaic, the first multimedia Web browser, in February 1994, and we saw the future. We were two years ahead of Bill Gates. I sought and received NBMA approval to start an Internet Special Interest Group (SIG) in December 1994, and we had our first SIG meeting in January 1995. It was the first Internet SIG of any organization in the Bay Area. I have dedicated this book to my friends and colleagues from NBMA, many of whom were pioneers in making the Web useful to people and businesses. Thanks for a great experience lasting many years.

Also thanks to Carole McClendon at Waterside Productions, my agent, who always does a great job, and to Jacqueline Flynn and the people at AMACOM, including Mike Sivilli, Kama Timbrell, Bob Chen, and Andy Ambraziejus, who have contributed to the success of the *Smart Way* series of eBay books. Thanks as well to Stephen Ingle of WordCo, who has helped with the copy editing, proofreading, and indexing of the books.

Again thanks to my wife Lani, daughter Brook, and son Tommy, who continue to support my time-consuming writing habit. They deserve a round of applause.

Neither eBay nor my books would be successful without the activities—sometimes courageous activities—of the many eBay entrepreneurs, who each day set the retail trends for the new century. Many have contributed indirectly if not directly to this book. Thanks.

Finally, I don't want to overlook the people at eBay and the people working at the many vendors that serve the eBay industry and provide products, services, and software. They have all done a great job. Thanks, folks.

I

Introduction to eBay Marketing Plus

1

Introduction

If you are reading this book, you are assumed to:

1. Be an experienced eBay seller.

2. Operate an eBay retail business full-time, or a substantial eBay retail business part-time.

3. Know all the basic facts of eBay retail life, including: bidding, selling (auctioning), paying and receiving payment, shipping, digital photography, the feedback system, and the like.

4. Have found your eBay retail niche and are selling well.

5. Want to increase your eBay sales volume.

What Increase?

One way to increase your sales is to increase your product line and sell more products. This book considers that strategy in Chapter 19 on Cross-Selling. However, that idea is not the primary theme of this book. This book focuses on increasing your sales in your existing line of products.

In *eBay Business the Smart Way* Second Edition, I offer the proposition that whatever you sell, marketing takes 50 percent of your time, effort, and money. Although this is a general rule and may not be applicable to your business, it always surprises me how universal it is. The rule fits a whole range of products and services from legal work to selling shoes. Unfortunately, marketing and advertising are expensive. The question is, Can you beat the rule? The answer is, not often.

That's what makes eBay so exciting. It's one way you can actually beat the rule. In a competitive business world where marketing is the name of the game, eBay actually lets you beat the 50-percent rule. Why? Because eBay does your marketing for you. It's eBay's marketing and eBay's brand that bring buyers to the eBay auctions and to eBay Stores. All you have to do is become an eBay seller and pay the modest eBay fees to take part in this huge and amazing new marketplace.

eBay Plus

This book assumes that you know that eBay is a great new marketplace with plenty of opportunity for anybody who wants to partake, and that I would be preaching to the choir if I included a couple of paragraphs touting eBay. The question for you then becomes, Where can I get more of the same? That is, where can you market your products in such a way that 50 percent of your time, effort, and money will not be required to generate sales? That's a great question, and this book devotes a lot of space to answering it.

Data

A significant portion of this book considers using your existing data to increase your sales. This is a concept particularly appropriate to the Web. With the recent emergence of new Web marketplaces, this idea has become possible, practical, and compelling. So, let's explore it briefly.

DATAFEED MARKETING

Your listing information for your eBay auction ads or for your eBay Store ads consists of data. This information is stored in a database. That database is Turbo Lister or whatever other software or auction management service you might use for processing your listings.

eBay Stores are, in effect, catalogs. Each Store is a catalog for the owner's products. That's easy to see and understand. What's perhaps a little less obvious is that eBay itself is a catalog. It's a huge catalog with many different categories, but a catalog nonetheless. What brings the catalog to life is the data that individual sellers submit for their items to be included for sale on eBay. The data for an item fills a template which is essentially a catalog webpage but something that we call an eBay auction ad.

Casual sellers that sell items on eBay submit their auction-ad data directly to eBay. They don't necessarily retain any of the data. However, that's not true for retail sellers, as they typically have too many products to submit to eBay individually. Most eBay retail sellers use auction-management software, such as eBay's Turbo Lister or Andale's Lister Pro, to store their listing data. It is the software which submits the data to eBay to create the auction ads (fills up the auction-ad webpage templates). As a result, even though eBay has the data, the individual eBay retailers retain the data too. The data stays with the software they use such as Turbo Lister or Lister Pro.

In fact, many eBay retailers sell the same products over and over again and reuse their auction ads. Because eBay retailers retain the data for their auction ads, the question becomes, Where else can I use this data to sell products other than eBay and eBay Stores?

The answer to that question is simply that there are other marketplaces on the Web that will accept your data for catalog entries. One way to describe this process is to say that you provide data to another marketplace in order to fill up (populate) catalog pages in that marketplace. Let's call this a "datafeed." Thus, what we are talking about is datafeed marketing. That is, let's see how many places (marketplaces) we can send your data to populate catalog pages and sell more of your products.

There are plenty of places to send data to populate catalog entries or pages. Most of them cost money. Consequently, a more specific question is, Where can I send my datafeed to sell my products cost-effectively, that is, profitably? And, of course, if you can find places to send your datafeed for free and sell more products, that's about as cost-effective as you can get. It takes very little effort and expense to send the datafeed.

Labor for Money

This book is not just about marketing on the Web. Generally speaking, it costs just as much money to market on the Web as it does to market offline. Although you cannot buy a television Super Bowl ad on the Web, you can nonetheless spend a lot of money pretty quickly. Most eBay businesses do not have large advertising budgets. Therefore, the main focus of a book about marketing for eBay retailers has to be marketing *cost-effectively*, and also, marketing that is inexpensive.

The one advantage that you do have on the Web that you don't have offline is that you can substitute your labor for money. Offline newspapers, magazines, television stations, and radio stations want cash for advertising. It would be a rare deal wherein you would substitute your labor for cash and perform some services for a newspaper, magazine, television station, or radio station in return for advertising. Consequently, offline marketing and advertising tends to drain your cash.

Online, however, many of the marketing and advertising techniques only require skills that anyone can learn. Then too, everyone has access to the Internet. Anyone can publish a website inexpensively through a host Internet Service Provider (ISP). There is plenty of work to do for which skilled people get paid money. But you can learn to do much of that work yourself and save yourself spending the money. In doing so, you will be substituting your time for money.

It Takes a Lot of Time

But make no mistake, doing your own marketing on the Web takes a tremendous amount of time.

Operating a small business requires a substantial amount of time and effort. This is not a new idea. This is called sweat equity. And sweat equity works on the Web as well as offline. Moreover, sweat equity works for doing your own marketing on the Web. As a result, an eBay retail business presents a great opportunity for doing one's marketing, at least partially, with sweat equity. That's great news for those pulling themselves up by their bootstraps in their eBay retail businesses.

Unfortunately, even eBay retail entrepreneurs have a limited amount of time. Think of your time as an extra bank account with money (in regard to running an eBay retail business) but one with a limited amount of money. There are only so many hours in the day. So, the question becomes the same as the question for money, Which means of marketing are the most cost-effective? In other words, How do I get the most for my time?

Note that based on the discussion above, this book's definition of cost-effective includes the consideration of both your time and your money. In other words, cost-effectiveness doesn't mean just money alone. Because you can substitute your time for money on the Web, cost-effectiveness means getting the most for the least time spent. Indeed, the goal of this book is to lead you to cost-effective means of marketing. Thus, I will set forth some ideas that I think are highly cost-effective. In addition, I will cover some traditional means of marketing on the Web to determine how cost-effective they really are. So, the emphasis of this book is on saving your time and your money.

Collectibles

In ten years collectibles went from 95 percent of eBay sales to less than 6 percent of eBay sales.

Today, however, there is another transformation going on. eBay is becoming the cornerstone of ecommerce. Rather than just another market locale in a vast metropolis of online commerce, eBay has become the gateway to consumer ecommerce itself. Probably 70 percent of the retail online consumer commerce is initiated on either eBay, Google, or Froogle. Tomorrow maybe 80 percent. Because you can use the same product data for eBay auctions, eBay Stores, Froogle, and other online marketplaces, I call this new phenomenon the *datafeed marketplace*.

Note that I have no statistical data to back up the percentages stated. They are my own rough estimates.

Out of the Box

The box is eBay and eBay Stores, and I'm asking you to think out of the box, to use a popular phrase. Let's put this in perspective. First, I believe that eBay and eBay Stores are fabulous opportunities. Many of the techniques this book covers will help you do a better job of marketing and selling your products on eBay. Indeed, beyond eBay there are seemingly attractive online-marketing techniques that I believe are not cost-effective for most online retailers. Part of the purpose of this book is to warn you of those. But beyond eBay there are also great opportunities for additional sales at little additional cost. So, the question is, Why not?

Why not expand your marketing activities beyond eBay? The combination of eBay, eBay Stores, and Froogle is an extraordinary combination marketplace that you should not overlook.

The Box Is Bigger Than We Thought

Is it really thinking out of the box to consider ways to sell your eBay retail products online other than through eBay? Probably not, primarily because there's a new box. The new box is the datafeed marketplace, and eBay is right in the middle of what's emerging. As an active eBay business, you are right in the center of this new phenomenon, and you don't have to reach far to take advantage of it. That is, you don't have to do much to seek and realize sales beyond eBay. And soon doing so will seem a normal part of your business.

Yet, there's more to increasing eBay sales than it seems. There are techniques you can use on eBay itself. There are traditional Web-marketing techniques to consider carefully. And there are new marketing techniques that promise to be productive and cost-effective. There are even traditional Web-marketing techniques to be avoided by small businesses. This book is not just a compendium of online marketing techniques. It is about cost-effective marketing.

Look! I don't have eBay stock. I'm not employed by eBay. And I'm not beholden to eBay in any way. I just tell it like I see it. And what I see is a new way to rev up your eBay business outside of eBay—a cost-effective new way.

eBay has gone through a significant evolution in its short ten years of life. It started in 1995 as a collectibles marketplace operating during a time when it had little public recognition. In 1998 it emerged as an institutional marketplace for used goods during a time when it was mistakenly perceived as a large flea market and a passing fad. (I have been comparing eBay to the New York Stock Exchange since 1998. And the *Wall Street Journal* finally acknowledged eBay as an institution in 2004.)

About 2002, eBay emerged as an industry—more than just an institution. Vendors had materialized that provided everything from auction-management software to eBay consignment-store franchises. eBay itself was relegated to being the cornerstone of a larger phonomenon. During this period eBay transformed into a more general marketplace that included huge volumes of new merchandise and items sold at fixed prices as well as the traditional used goods. eBay advertises so much and appears so often in Google-Froogle that eBay and Google-Froogle pratically overlap. I haven't heard anyone speak of eBay as an industry, but a visit to the next annual eBay Live conference will make it clear to you that it is.

Yes, the box is bigger than we thought. So, let's think both in the box and out of the box to find out what we can understand.

Cost-Effectiveness Review

Because the cost-effectiveness factor is so important for small businesses, this book includes a cost-effectiveness review at the end of each appropriate chapter. The purpose of such a review is to determine how cost-effective a particular online-marketing technique is and in what circumstances the technique works well. Some of the techniques covered in this book, contrary to popular belief, are not very cost-effective.

They are techniques you will want to avoid using. Yet in certain circumstances, you may find them worthwhile to use.

The cost-effectiveness review takes into account your time, too, not just your money. You can substitute your time for money in marketing on the Web, but you still have a limited amount of time. Thus, carefully considering the amount of your time and money required by any particular online-marketing technique is an excellent way for you to get the most out of your overall marketing effort.

Tracking Sales

It's great to discuss cost-effectiveness. And this book assumes that if you can promote your products easily at low cost or at no cost, that it is cost-effective marketing. That may not be true.

In the next chapter, on the datafeed marketplace, the ideas of relevancy and significance are added to the analysis. Is the marketplace where you seek to sell your merchandise relevant to what you sell? Is it a marketplace that has significant traffic that can be expected to generate significant sales for you? But again, although these two additional considerations will help you make better decisions, they do not ensure success.

The proof is in the pudding, as they say. You try something to see if it works. If it does, you're a genius. If it doesn't, you're a dunce. More importantly, if it works you make money. If it doesn't work, you waste time, effort, and money for little gain, or perhaps even a loss. However, the only way you can know is to track your sales. You need to know where your sales are coming from in order to evaluate your various marketing programs.

By the Way

As many people have said, success is measured in how many failures you experience before you finally succeed. So don't be discouraged by a failed marketing effort. Try and try again. You will become the marketing expert in your niche.

In Chapter 26, this book introduces analytic techniques you can use to analyze your sales. This is the last word in marketing. Do your various marketing efforts produce sales? If so, which are most worthwhile? Only you can discover this. This is the ultimate measure of cost-effectiveness and is one that's personal to you and your online retail business.

Thus, you can understand that the Cost-Effectiveness Reviews in the appropriate chapters are generalized. Only you can determine which marketing techniques work for your products, and you can do so by using the sales-analysis techniques in Chapter 26.

Conclusion

Beyond giving you a specialized book on Web marketing for eBay retailers, this book is unique because it stresses the idea of datafeed marketing, a new idea in Web marketing. This is not only a new idea, but it is an idea specifically appropriate to eBay retail businesses. Therefore, a substantial portion of this book will be devoted to datafeed marketing.

The good news is that datafeed marketing can increase your markets by 30, 50, or 100 percent with little additional effort or expense above and beyond what you already spend to run your eBay retail business. The bad news is that to embrace and understand this Web-marketing technique, one has to understand how databases work.

Understanding how databases work is not the same as being able to create, program, and operate databases. That is best left to database programmers. Nonetheless, you need to understand that databases are at the core of virtually every business program and that understanding databases is important to you in your role as an eBay retailer. You will soon notice that there is a lot of information on databases in this book. Understanding databases can make money for you.

There are a lot of ways to use Web marketing to expand your eBay retail sales. Without an unlimited budget, though, you have to allocate your time and money intelligently. This book shows you how to do just that, increase your retail sales intelligently. That is, this book shows you how to build your eBay traffic the smart way.

If You Have an Idea

I will be happy to hear from you at jt@sinclair.com if you have a marketing idea that you think I should include in future editions the book. I operate a website for eBay retail sellers, Bayside Business, at *http://baysidebusiness.com*. You can visit that website for additional information and for updates on the book. In addition, you can sign up for my eBay newsletter delivered by email by going to the AMACOM website *http://www.amanet.org/books/index.htm* or the Bayside Business website. My former website, Book-Center.com, will now get you to BaysideBusiness.com.

If you are interested in expanding your sales through selling abroad, you may be able to establish relationships with business-people in other countries through Trade Affiliates (*http://tradeaffiliates.com*). This is a directory that I have initiated to help eBay retailers establish contacts in other countries in order to seek mutually beneficial trade arrangements.

2

The New Datafeed Marketplaces

Talk about cost-effectiveness. It doesn't get any better than this. If you can send a datafeed—easy to do—to an additional Web marketplace to create catalog entries, and if it doesn't cost anything, this process is about as cost-effective as you can get. When the additional marketplace is Froogle (free at the time this book went to press), you can potentially increase your sales by a huge amount with nominal effort and expense. What a deal!

This is something you can't afford to overlook if you're serious about your eBay retail business. Consequently, this book thoroughly covers this aspect of building your retail traffic.

How It Works

You already have data for your eBay auction listings and eBay Store listings (e.g., in Turbo Lister). That data fills a webpage template with information and becomes the eBay auction ad or the eBay Store catalog webpage (ad). Why not use the same data for other online listings and catalogs such as Froogle or Yahoo Shopping? In fact, you can do this easily. Just take a subset (i.e., a portion) of the data you already have and send it to the website (e.g., Froogle) where you want to sell your items. You *export* the data to the target website. Another way of saying this is that you *provide a datafeed* to the target website.

Froogle and Yahoo

Google is the leading search engine with a market share that's over 50 percent. Yahoo runs a distant second with a market share that's about 20 percent. Both Google and Yahoo have created strictly retail searches (searchs that return only products for sale). Google calls its special search Froogle. Yahoo calls its special search Yahoo Shopping. From your point of view, you can send a datafeed to each and expand your sales. Froogle is currently free. However, Yahoo Shopping charges for each click-through and can be expensive.

Froogle is a huge opportunity for you (see Figure 2.1). Clearly it's the biggest and most cost-effective marketing and sales opportunity you have online in addition to eBay and eBay Stores. If you pass it up, you're leaving money on the table.

Go to *http://www.google.com* and click on the Froogle link and start your search, or go to *http://www.froogle.com* and search for an item you want to buy. Froogle will deliver a series of item listings to you, in effect a catalog. You simply decide where you want to buy, and one click will get you to the selling website. It's simple and effective.

Figure 2.1 Froogle looks a lot like Google. ©2004 Google

For a long time many people have been using Google to shop. Since it's impossible to track sales through Google, no one knows how many sales are made through Google. My best guess is that the sales volume is equal to if not greater than eBay. Unfortunately, to sell effectively on Google, your website has to be found by the Google search engine. Read Chapter 16 to learn about getting found by the search engines. It may not be cost-effective for you.

With Froogle, however, your website doesn't have to get found. You provide a datafeed to Froogle, and your listings (items) will appear in the Froogle catalog (webpages). It's simple, and it's free.

Froogle started its beta test in December of 2002. Yahoo copied it soon thereafter with Yahoo Product Search, which was in beta until the fall of 2003. Yahoo Product Search was free to retailers while in beta.

Beta Testing

A beta test is the last test of a hardware or software product used under normal conditions before it officially goes on the market for sale to the public. Beta testing is usually done using a select group of actual customers. In the case of both Froogle and Yahoo Shopping, the beta test was done with public participation.

When Yahoo Product Search emerged from beta in September 2003 and started operation officially as a feature of Yahoo, it was renamed Yahoo Shopping. Yahoo then started charging retailers for listings with a substantial fee for every click-through on an item.

Click-Throughs

In Yahoo Shopping, each time a potential buyer clicks on your item, you are charged a fee. It wouldn't be so bad if each click-through resulted in a sale. But a high ratio of click-throughs to sales can make Yaho Shopping an expensive way to sell at retail on the Web, unless you sell items with a generous margin.

Froogle completed beta in March of 2004 at which time it officially became a feature of Google. Froogle is still free for retailers, even though it's not in beta any longer. Although still in its infancy, Froogle is destined to grow in popularity comparable to its parent Google. So long as it's free, it's a great opportunity for cost-effective retail sales.

Other Marketplaces

Froogle and Yahoo aren't the only datafeed marketplace opportunities. Here is a sampling of others:

BizRate, *http://www.bizrate.com*

BottomDollar.com, *http://www.bottomdollar.com*

Calibex, *http://www.calibex.com*

C/NET Shopper, *http://google-cnet.com.com/ 2001-1_9-0.html?tag=tab*

Digital Saver, *http://www.digitalsaver.com*

EveryPrice, *http://www.everyprice.com*

Interactive Reviews, *http://www.interactivereviews.com*

MySimon, *http://www.mysimon.com*

NexTag, *http://www.nextag.com*

PriceArrow, *http://www.pricearrow.com*

PriceFish, *http://www.pricefish.com*

PriceGrabber, *http://www.pricegrabber.com*

PriceHead, *http://www.pricehead.com*

PriceScan, *http://www.pricescan.com*

ShopCartUSA, *http://www.shopcartusa.com*

Shopping.com, *http://www.shopping.com*

Shopzilla, *http://www.shopzilla.com*

Each is a little different. They each take different subsets of data and charge different fees. Most are comparison websites. Some may be affiliates of others; that is, a datafeed to one may result in a presence on others. This is a fast changing ecommerce environment, and you will want to ivestigate each possibility to determine what it can do for you.

Google and Retailer Comparison Websites

Google remains an important online shopping gateway and will probably outperform (in retail sales) its new invention Froogle for a few years. However, Google has to find your website—it doesn't take a datafeed—requiring a serious commitment of your time, effort, and money to get found. One way to sneak into Google is via the comparison websites.

What's a retailer comparison website? It's a website that compares the price of a specific product as purchased from different retailers. It also compares the buyer ratings of the retailers. Each retailer typically must pay a fee to have their products included in the comparisons. The data regarding the products is submitted via a datafeed.

The comparison websites buy ads on Google, which appear along the right side of the screen when a Google user seeks information about a specific product. Thus, as a retailer comparison website participant, you get prime advertising at a reasonable cost.

The catch is that if your price isn't the lowest (in the comparison), your chances of making a sale are not high. However, the comparison websites also enable buyers to rate sellers. Many sellers have low ratings due to substandard customer service. If you provide first rate customer service, your chances of making a sale will increase substantially, even when you don't offer the lowest price.

If you shop much online, you will recognize many of the above listed websites. The question is not whether you should participate in online marketplaces other than eBay. The question is which websites can increase your sales cost-effectively. Froogle is a no-brainer because it's free. Are there others like Froogle?

This book can't answer that question for you. With over 22 million products for sale each week on eBay and an unknown number for sale elsewhere on the Web, it becomes difficult to generalize about where on the Web your products will sell well. Only your retail knowledge about your own products and your research regarding places for you to sell on the Web via a datafeed will lead you to make cost-effective choices about selling in new marketplaces.

II

The Basics

3

Customer Service

When you can afford to spend a lot of money to build your brand, there's a difference between customer service and branding. When you have little money for advertising, as is true of many eBay retail businesses, for all practical purposes there isn't much difference between customer service and branding. It's your superb customer service that will build your brand both on eBay and other places online.

Successful online retailers offer very good customer service. In fact, great customer service, with Amazon.com in the lead, has become the hallmark of online commerce. The word quickly gets around the

Internet about retailers who do not treat their customers well. For example, the comparative shopping directories show not only the price of products but consumer ratings on the vendors selling the products. Therefore, I conclude—although branding experts might quibble about this—that for building an eBay retail business, customer service is almost synonymous with branding.

What Is Customer Service?

Customer service is all of the things you do to make a buyer's purchase as effortless and convenient as possible. It's also the things you do to assist a buyer in effortlessly getting off to a good start in using the products you sold.

There is an strong emphasis on customer service in all the other eBay books I have written. So why include a chapter on it in this book? Simply put, customer service is so important that no book on marketing on the Web should be without a chapter on it. This chapter is brief and doesn't dwell on what I've covered in my other books, but at least it's here as a reminder near the beginning of the book that customer service is crucial to good marketing. After all, the most likely prospective buyer is someone who is already your satisfied customer.

Here is a short list of some of the basic practices that require your attention in your own retailing organization so you can provide first rate customer service:

- Well-organized business procedures
- Timely communication with customers
- Easy checkout
- Quick fulfillment

The above list shows that if you are well organized to conduct your retail business in a professional and business-like manner, such an approach will go a long ways towards providing excellent customer service. What makes everything work, in addition to the list above, is your own personal attention to detail and your employees' personal attention to detail. In a word, no system operates without somebody adjusting it and tweaking it everyday to make it work well.

Personal Touch

The other thing that makes a retail sales system work well is your personal attention to problems (and your employees' personal attention to problems). The problems of which I am speaking are the problems buyers have that only you can solve. For most products, the routine transactions do not have problems. But inevitably buyers have problems with some products. It's up to you as a seller to make sure that those problems are minimal, are handled expeditiously, and make the experience of resolving such problems seem effortless and convenient for buyers.

Cost-Effectiveness Review

Customer service is expensive and it takes time. It's one of those rare marketing techniques that is expensive and does take time but is nonetheless very worthwhile. It's a must-do. Your business will never reach its maximum volume and profitability without good customer service, and your retail business could very well fail, particularly on the Web, if you do not provide good customer service.

4

Copy Writing

What is copy? Copy is the text you find in advertising, particularly text for catalogs and direct mail solicitations. In other words, it's the kind of text you want for your eBay auction ads and eBay Store catalog webpages. Copy writing is not necessarily hype like the short phrases in magazine advertisements. It's persuasive writing in sentences and paragraphs.

Copy writing is an art. Those who do it well get paid handsomely. Good copy writing sells merchandise. Can you expect to write your auction ads like a professional copy writer? Probably not. (I know I can't.) Yet you want to do the best job you can. It ultimately means more money in your pocket. Thus, it pays to learn a few writing guidelines that can substantially improve your copy writing.

Guidelines

What follows are some basic writing guidelines. These guidelines focus on the writing, not the content. Good writing is the first step. Clearly communicating information about products is the goal. Once you have mastered basic writing skills, you can read a book on copy writing and focus on content—that is, writing persuasive content.

Book on Copy Writing

A book on copy writing, besides stressing good writing, will also teach the art of pursuasion. To persuade, you need to tie the features of the product to the benefits they will bring to the customer.

Organize

Organize your thoughts before you start writing. If you have time, outline what you're going to write. As they say, a good story has a beginning, a middle, and an end. So does a good eBay auction ad.

In effect, you tell the story of your product. The story affects the purchasing decision of the buyer. If the story rambles on without any point or is just a list of specifications, it won't have a lot of impact. As a result, the prosepctive buyer may remain undecided. If you write a coherent story and give it a point, it will lead a potential buyer to make a purchasing decision, and you will have achieved your purpose.

What's the point to make in your copy? *Here's the product (describe it). Here's what it can do. And here's what it can do for you.* If you can get a potential buyer to make a decision—doesn't matter whether it's to buy or not to buy—generally your bids will increase (and the winning bids will be higher).

Here are some priorities for an organized ad:

1. Full information on the product (e.g., specifications)

2. Full information on the condition of the product (if not new)

3. What the product can do

4. Benefits of the product to a buyer

5. Request to bid (or to buy)

With over 22 million items for sale every week, I can only give general guidelines in a chapter on copy writing. Each product is different, and some products may require special treatment for copy writing. But good organization in your writing will take you a long way down the road to writing solid and effective copy.

Make It Long

Remember, the Web is an informational medium. There is no shortage of space to tell the story of your product. This is not a classified ad where you pay by the word. You can use as many words as you need to, and the price for the space is the same.

In a mail order catalog, the descriptions of products are short because space is limited, but you will notice that the descriptions are much longer and more informational than in the hype of a magazine or newspaper display ad.

In direct mail solicitations (junk mail), the descriptions of products are particularly long and informational because even more space is available for one price. Good copy writers take advantage of the space available to make a thorough sales pitch to the reader. They focus on the benefits of the product's features to the buyer. The reading space usually consists of whatever paper the seller can cram into one ounce (the smallest unit of weight and the lowest postage). That's the equivalent of four 8.5 x 11 sheets.

Direct mail is very effective. We tend to discount this fact, because we don't read direct mail in which we are not interested. But when a solicitation arrives in the mail for a product we happen to want or need that day, we read it. And often the solicitation is quite enticing.

Generally eBay product descriptions should be somewhere in length between a catalog description and a direct mail solicitation. You can justify writing longer ads for more expensive or more complex products. Your time is the real limitation here. The space is available.

Keep It Short

Having told you to make it long, I'm going to tell you to keep it short. What's going on here? In this case, focus on your actual writing, not the amount of content. Use short words, short sentences, and short paragraphs. More people understand—and are comfortable reading— short words rather than long words. Short sentences read faster and are more understandable than long sentences. And reading short paragraphs goes faster and is less tedious than reading long paragraphs. So, write as much as you need to, but write it in short chunks with simple words.

Then too, you don't have to use the all space available, which is practically unlimited. The objective is to say what you need to about a product to give a prospective buyer enough solid information to make a buying decision, no more and no less. For some products that may be two sentences and for other products it may be twenty or even two hundred sentences. Say what you need to and end it there.

Make It Personal

Don't try to make your writing conform to some pretentious stereotype. For instance, you don't want your ad to sound like a lawyer wrote it. No one will read it. Write in your own voice. Give your writing some personality. In other words, you don't want to make your writing abstract and impersonal.

We all talk with numerous people every day, and we differentiate them by their personalities. We are very skilled at doing so. We feel comfortable with information that has a human voice. We get bored with or even become suspicious of impersonal communications.

That doesn't mean that you have to overwhelm prosepctive buyers with your down-home dialog and charm, but it does mean that you can be yourself when you write your eBay auction ads. Write naturally as you would talk. That's the best way to make your writing personal, and that's the best way you can write.

Use Action Verbs

People are much more interested in *who did what to whom* than they are in *what is*. Use action verbs wherever possible and avoid the passive.

Action (active): John taped the package.

Inactive: The package is taped.

Passive: The package was taped by John.

Action moves reading along and gives power to the message. The passive puts readers to sleep. It's not always possible to write with action verbs when copy writing, but use action verbs as much as possible.

Use Plain Language

This is similar to keeping it short. Use short words instead of long words wherever you can, and your language will be plainer. More people understand short words, and short words are easier to read for everyone. But it's more than keeping your words short. Don't use jargon or technical language.

Your object here is to present information on the product to the greatest number of prosepctive buyers. Your objective is not to inform readers that you are a member of the in-group (associated with the product) by tossing around technical terms and jargon. When you use plain language, you focus your message on the product and on informing readers. When you use lots of jargon, you are, in effect, focusing the message on yourself and leaving many readers baffled.

Sure, for many products you need to include technical information, product specifications (containing technical information), and industry jargon. But keep it to a minimum, and when you use anything but plain language, explain it to your readers.

You can argue that for certain technical items, the only bidders will be prospective buyers who will understand the industry jargon. I don't buy that argument. For instance, I'm not an electrician or an electronics technician, but I bought a voltmeter a few years back. It was a one-project purchase, and I wanted to pay the lowest price possible. Yet I needed to be assured that I bought the right voltmeter to get the job done. Jargon didn't help me—it hindered me—in making my purchasing decision. In fact, I couldn't find an informative eBay ad for a voltmeter among the many auction ads on eBay for voltmeters. Consequently, I bought the voltmeter offline at Radio Shack.

Don't Use Vague Modifiers

Modifiers such as *very*, *reasonably*, *basically*, *real*, and *great* add little to your writing. Avoid using them and weed them out when you edit.

Don't Use Abbreviations

We all live in our own little world. The abbreviations we use are self-evident. The problem is that only a few of our compatriots understand them. The remainder of the people on planet Earth are confounded by such abbreviations.

Originally eBay was a small group of collectibles traders. First, one hundred. Then one thousand. Then ten thousand, etc. They developed a set of abbreviations that most early participants understood. Today there are over 100 million registered eBay users. Collectibles account for less than 6 percent of eBay's volume. How many eBay members today understand the traditional eBay abbreviations? My guess is that 99.5 percent don't. Yet you see more abbreviations in eBay ads you do in a collegiate dictionary. And that's just eBay abbreviations.

Products carry their own set of abbreviations. Don't use those abbreviations either. Many potential buyers just won't understand what you're saying. They won't bid. The bidding will be thinner. And the selling price will be lower.

I Don't Mind Being Dumb

I don't mind being dumb. When I read an abbreviation I don't understand (often) in an eBay ad for something in which I'm interested in buying, I email the seller for an explanation of the abbreviation. If everyone did this, many sellers would be overwhelmed with email. Instead, such sellers just lose potential customers unknowingly.

Edit Yourself

I could tell you to have everything you write edited by someone, and that would be good advice. Unfortunately, few eBay retailers would do it. After all, they are busy business people. Where are they going to find the time to get someone to edit their copy?

Still, you can edit yourself. It's best when you can let a lot of time go by between edits. Two weeks is better than two days. But even when you can't let much time go by, at least edit your copy writing yourself anyway.

Edit for spelling and grammar and also eliminate words you don't need. If you get rid of words that aren't necessary to what you're saying, you make your writing easier to read and more powerful.

When you sell the same items routinely, you will have the chance to edit your copy each time you post another auction ad. This gives you the opportunity to edit until it you get it just right. Once you get it right, the copy will keep on selling.

Live Without Fear

You can't worry about spelling, grammar, and structure. If you did, you'd never post your first eBay auction ad. Do the best job you can and get the ad up. However, this point of view doesn't mean you shouldn't strive to improve your copy writing. Keep at it. Practice makes perfect, particularly when it comes to writing.

Use what's available. That means spell-checkers, grammar-checkers, and even software that helps you structure your writing. I couldn't pass a middle school spelling test to save my life. Yet a spell checker keeps me out of trouble—most of the time.

Books

Read the classics on clear writing. They're easy, and they're fun to read:

The Elements of Style, Strunk and White, Kt Publishing

On Writing Well, William Zinsser, Harper Collins Publishers

For more in-depth instruction specifically on copywriting try:

The Copywriter's Handbook, Robert W. Bly, Owl Books

A more difficult book but one worth slogging through if you're well motivated to improve your writing is:

Style, Toward Clarity and Grace, Joseph M. Williams, University of Chicago Press

Catalog retailers spend a lot of time and effort to make their catalogs read well and sell merchandise well. By improving the writing for your auction ad copy, you can increase your sales too.

Cost-Effectiveness Review

Good copy writing takes time. Time's not money, but it's still a finite commodity. You have to write your copy (or hire it done). You might as well learn to do a good job since you need to write copy one way or another. But you need to conserve your time too. Perhaps the best approach is to develop a strategy that limits the amount of time you spend writing. Here are some things you can do:

1. Give priority for writing good copy to products you will sell again and again.

2. Give priority to your most expensive products.

3. Use links to manufacturers' websites to supplement your product information wherever possible. In other words, if a manufacturer provides it, use it. Don't reinvent the wheel.

4. Copy product literature from packages or product flyers wherever possible. (You may be violating a copyright, but this is a widespread practice on eBay. I don't recommend that you do this, but if you do, limit it to one-time sales. For repeat sales of products, write your own copy, particularly for eBay Stores and Froogle.)

The trouble with doing a cost-effectiveness review regarding copy writing is that the cost-effectiveness analysis applies only to that portion of the time it takes you to do a good job over and above the time it takes you to do a mediocre job. It's this extra time that you need to consider in your cost-effectiveness evaluation. Since you will improve with learning and practice, you will become more efficient in writing good copy over time. Considering the importance of good copy, I have to conclude that competent copy writing is time well spent on marketing your products.

5

Writing Titles

What are titles? They are the headings above eBay auctions. Why does this chapter come after the chapter on writing copy for auction ads? (Titles precede auction ads in eBay webpages.) That's a good question. It's my perception that you can write a better title after you've written an auction ad than before. After all, you have all the product information right in front of you, well organized and well written. Writing the title is straightforward and easy.

Writing to Be Found

Writing titles is not for selling and not necessarily for marketing. It's not copy writing. It's for getting found by the eBay search engine. That's its sole function. (Of course the striving to get found is itself a marketing technique.) Consequently, titles are much easier to write than copy for auction ads.

Simple and Direct

What does a title for one of your products need to do? A few important ideas should prove useful. The title should:

- Completely identify the item
- Contain appropriate keywords for the eBay search engine
- Indicate whether the item is new, and if used, indicate the condition

It's that simple. Don't try to make it more complicated. Notice that I didn't say the following:

- Attract attention
- Hook prospective buyers
- Start the sales process

Indeed, the need to use hype is a misconception that many eBay sellers—and not a few eBay authors—make. They're mistaken or not clear about the purpose of the title.

Let's say you are selling a FastAction XT-90 digital camcorder, a well known brand and model. Prospective buyers get to the list of digital camcorders via the eBay search (i.e., keywords = *digital* and *camcorder*) or by working their way down through the category tree to the subsection *Camcorders*. If a potential buyer is looking for a FastAction XT-90, you want him to be able to immediately spot your title in the very long list of titles for camcorders.

The following title says it all:

FastAction XT-90 digital camcorder new

A prosepctive buyer can skim the list quickly and spot this title easily. You've done your job well. Once prospective buyers have found your ad, they will skim or read your ad copy. That's where you make your sales pitch.

Anything that detracts from potential buyers finding your auction ad easily will result in fewer bidders and ultimately lower sales prices. For instance, look at some of the following titles:

FASTACTION XT-90 DIGITAL CAMCORDER NEW

@WOW@ Fabulous Digital Camcorder***

!!! XT-90 great FastAction digital camcorder in the box!!!

FastAction camcorder - award winning - new

The first is in all caps, which is hard to read. The second uses characters that interfere with skimming. In addition, it doesn't say much that's concrete. It doesn't even include the brand or model number. The third is difficult to read due to the exclamation marks. "FastAction" and "XT-90" are separated and reversed and defy quick skimming. And what does "in the box" mean? It probably means new, but it could mean used but put back in the box. The fourth doesn't identify the camcorder as being digital or by model number. Someone looking for a digital camcorder could assume that it's an analog camcorder and would not be interested in it. "Award winning" is OK for an auction ad but not for a title; it doesn't help identify the product. These titles will cost you potential buyers.

There's no reason to make an art out of writing titles. They are straightforward. Just identify what's for sale using words that potential buyers will use to search.

Typesetting

Use standard typesetting like you find in easy-to-read books. Non-standard or haphazard typesetting distracts reading and interferes with skimming. See *eBay Business the Smart Way* Second Edition for more on proper typesetting.

Keywords

And let's have a few more words about keywords. If the title does not contain the appropriate keywords for an item, it won't work well no matter how well it is written and typeset. eBay buyers search for items on keywords. You need to determine what the keywords are for an item and include them in the title. Using the proper keywords is by itself a productive maketing technique, particularly when you do it routinely for all your auctions.

Often the proper keywords are identical to the descriptive words you use to provide information on your product. For instance, in the example earlier in the chapter, "camcorder" is a prime keyword. Then too, "camcorder" precisely describes the product.

Perhaps you can't spend a lot of time researching keywords when you sell just one item once. But when you plan to sell an item regularly, or when the item is a big-ticket product, you need to spend time figuring out what keyword(s) will sell the item best. Sometimes this isn't as easy as you want it to be, but it's worth doing. If a prospective buyer can't find your item through normal eBay searching, your item might as well be nonexistent.

Keywords and Titles

You can use the eBay keyword ads process (*https://ebay.admarket-place.net/ebay/servlet/ebay*) to discover effective keywords to use in your titles.

Getting found is the first step in the sales process. If your product doesn't get found, nothing happens.

Cost-Effectiveness Review

Writing titles does not take much time or energy. You don't have any choice; it has to be done. Just write the essentials that will help pontential buyers find what they're looking for. Include key search words. Follow standard typesetting guidelines so that potential buyers can skim without distraction. It's that easy.

6

Advanced Photography Techniques

My prior eBay books have provided basic information on taking acceptable photographs for eBay ads. For established eBay businesses, it's appropriate to do two things now. First, take better photographs. Second, establish an efficient workflow for your photographic processing. This chapters attempts to briefly cover both.

Unfortunately, it's difficult to help you do a good job of photographing clothes and then expect you to be able to do a good job photographing jewelry too. Due to limited space, this chapter will be general. However, I am scheduled to write and publish *eBay Photography the Smart*

Way in the spring of 2005 to provide you with detailed instructions on photographing a variety of diverse items. Stanley Livingston, a professional product photographer with 40 years experience, is the co-author of the upcoming book. In the meanwhile, this chapter will get you headed in the right direction.

Why Good Photographs?

Wouldn't you be embarrassed if someone bought a $300 set of chairs from you on eBay and turned around and sold them on eBay for $550? The difference is that you took one dull photograph of one of the chairs slightly out of focus, and the buyer (who subsequently sold for a profit) took a half-dozen dazzling sharp photographs, some showing close-ups of the detailing on the chairs.

There are people who buy items on eBay from sellers who have done a careless job of photography and then sell for a profit after taking careful photographs. OK, there are 22 million items for sale on eBay each week, and statistically there's bound to be opportunities for re-photographing for profit. That explains it. Or does it?

Stop and think what you get when you visit a retail shop in your locale. You can look at a product closely and even touch it. You can readily tell whether it will suit your purposes, and you can even see whether it is in the new condition you expect it to be. If used, you can quickly assess its condition. In addition, you can talk with a retail clerk to get more information about the product, although in today's retail environment of defunct customer service this doesn't always work well.

You don't need to smell it, unless it's food. You don't need to hear it, unless it's music. And you probably don't need to touch most things to make an intelligent buying decision. You rely primarily on your eyes and on product information. And that's why good photographs are so important online. They are a substitute for being there, for seeing with your own eyes.

We have all had experiences where we read a description of something. It sounded great. We ordered it (e.g., mail order). And when it arrived, it was way out of kilter with our expectations. We are very reluctant to repeat such an experience. That's why mail order catalogs have lots of great pictures (i.e., professional photographs).

Photographs are important! Good photographs in eBay ads bring good prices, and great photographs bring great prices. And a good tip regarding photographs is: As the price goes up, more is better. In other words, take your photographs carefully and skillfully, and for expensive items use multiple photographs in your auction ads.

Cameras

Because computer monitor resolution is so low, a two-megapixel digital camera is all you need to take good product photographs. A three-megapixel camera is a little better and gives you more room to crop your photographs and still maintain image quality. A four-megapixel is definitely overkill. With today's prices you can easily afford a digital camera that will get the job done for you.

Film Cameras

Film cameras are not recommended. Don't waste your time and money. Buy a digital camera if you don't have one already.

Many eBay business people will choose their digital cameras based on what they want and need for personal use. By all means, buy a six-megapixel DSLR (digital single-lens reflex) camera for $900 if you want to use it for photographing sunsets or whatever. It will do a good job of photographing products too.

You want to make sure that your digital camera has a macro (closeup) mode that gets you close to small items. Most do. However, if you choose a DSLR, you may have to get a special macro lens to take good closeups.

Prosumer Cameras

A good choice for high-quality personal use is one of the 7- or 8-megapixel prosumer cameras. They are similar to DSLRs but use only one lens and have good macro capability without requiring a special lens. The Minolta Dimage A2 and Nikon Coolpix 8800 are good examples. They cost a little bit less than low-end DSLRs.

Better Photographs

The focus in this chapter for better photographs is on lighting. The best lighting is a soft diffused source. Professional landscape photographers normally take their photographs at dawn or at dusk, the times when the sun provides a soft diffused light just before it comes over the eastern horizon or just after it disappears below the western horizon.

The harsh noonday sun produces shadows and glare (washout). The glare distracts and hides details, and the shadows also hide details in blackness. Indeed, professional photographers do their best outdoor work on lightly overcast days when the clouds are thick enough to diffuse sunlight but not thick enough to cause a depressing gray day.

And so it is in the studio. Diffused light is your goal. Diffused light will bring out details in your products without the glare and shadows, in most cases, which obscure such details. And it's the details that your customers want and need to make intelligent buying decisions.

Umbrellas

There are a variety of lighting devices that combine a light source with some sort of diffuser. The least expensive and most versatile are umbrella-tungsten-light sets. They are readily available at professional camera stores, in camera supply catalogs, and on the Web (e.g., eBay). They consist of an adjustable metal stand which holds a tungsten light source beaming into the underside of an umbrella. The unbrella reflects the light back highly diffused. You need two of these sets. They sell for as little as $120 each.

The umbrella sets work for large items as well as small and can be moved around easily as well as easily adjusted for height. With each new item you need to photograph, you can experiment with the umbrella lighting sets to eliminate glare and shadows. After some experience, setting up the lighting will become second nature. In fact, many similar items will require the same lighting, and you will not necessarily have to change the lighting from item to item.

A good place to start is to keep each of your lighting sources about 45 degrees off center. A third back light is also desirable in many circumstances but can be considered optional. (See Figure 6.1.) The third light must be an identical type of light to the others (i.e., tungsten) but does not necessarily have to use an umbrella. You can place the third behind the item but aimed at the background.

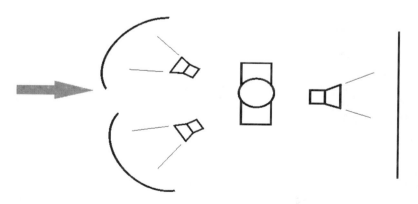

Figure 6.1 Lighting setup.

Surfaces

Naturally in your effort to eliminate glare and use soft light, you will want to eliminate highly reflective surfaces (e.g., mirrors) around the area where you take your photographs, particularly surfaces that will actually appear in a photograph (e.g., background).

Background

You need to use an inconspicuous background that does not detract attention from your item. For instance, a plain white or pastel bed-sheet can make a reasonable background, but a dark bedsheet or a bedsheet with a design does not make a good background.

Better than a bedsheet is a roll of photographic background paper. You can get a 54-inch-wide, 12-yard-long roll of paper for about $35 from a professional photo supply source. It also comes in 107-inch widths for about $60. The rack to hold the paper costs about $140. For an inexpensive substitute, use a broom stick hung from your ceiling by a cord at each end.

The use of the paper roll is to create an unobtrusive, non-glare background that flows from the vertical (your wall) to the horizontal (your table or floor) without showing the intersection (the line where your table or floor meets your wall). Make sure you choose a light color for product photography. Professional photographers use dark background paper rolls for photographing portraits, and such rolls are not usually appropriate for product photography.

Catalogs

If you can't find professional photography equipment and supplies (e.g., studio lights) locally, you can find them in the following photography-supply catalogs:

B&H Photo-Video-Audio, *http://www.bhphotovideo.com*, both online and printed catalogs

Calumet, *http://www.calumetphoto.com*, both online and printed catalogs

Freestyle Photographic Supplies, *http://www.freestylephoto.biz*, both online and printed catalogs

Porter's Camera Store, *http://porters.com*, both online and printed catalogs

When you photograph small items, a matte board, which sits on a tabletop, works well. You can purchase one from Cloud Dome at *http://www.clouddome.com* under the product name Infiniti Matte Board. (See Figure 6.2.)

Figure 6.2 Matte board for photographing small items. ©2004 Cloud Dome, Inc.

Light Boxes

For small items such as jewelry, you can use a light box. Light boxes typically contain diffused light sources that make your photography much easier than using a flash or natural light. The Cloud Dome (available at the Cloud Dome website referenced above) is an example of an inexpensive light-box-like device that diffuses natural light for easier high-quality photography. Most light boxes are considerably more expensive than the Cloud Dome and are much larger.

For choices in light boxes try:

Coloreal eBox, *http://www.ortery.com*

EZCube, *http://store.yahoo.com/greenbatteries-store*

Litestage, *http://www.litestage.com*

MK Digital Direct, *http://www.mkddigitaldirect.com*

Keep in mind that the whole point of using a light box is the use of diffused light. If you never photograph anything large, a light box can be your entire studio. For items about the size of an inkjet printer or larger, however, you will find even the larger light boxes to be inadequate. You will need umbrella lights instead.

White Balance

White balance is a setting on your digital camera that sets the camera to the temperature of the light you expect to use to take the next photograph. The temperature of light is measured in degrees Kelvin. Some examples are:

Blue sky	11,000K
Hazy sky	8,000K
Daylight at noon	5,500K
Typical daylight	5,000K
Studio flood lights	3,000 K
Household light bulbs	2,500K

Normally, your digital camera automatically sets the white balance for each photograph. If that works well for you, fine. If not, you may have to set the white balance yourself. Follow the instructions in your camera's user manual.

Not Brightness

Note that color temperature is not the same as brightness. Rather, it's the relative intensity of blue to red. Thus, household lights give you a yellowish light while a sunless blue sky gives you a bluish light.

You can get weird effects by mixing two tempertures of light. For instance, if you use tungsten light, make sure that you don't have a lot of daylight in the room. Stick with one kind of light (one temperature) and make sure the camera sets the white balance to that light.

Color Cast

Note, too, that some kinds of light (e.g., fluorescent) have a color cast. This is not a color temperature phenonmenon, but it affects color nonetheless.

Flash

Many eBay sellers use a flash to take their photographs. This is a down and dirty way to take acceptable photographs. Inevitably, however, you get glare from the flash in your photographs, which interferes with the visual detail you need to help sell your products. It also looks a little amateurish. You can take professional-looking photographs with a flash, but it requires techniques well beyond the scope of this book and is not recommended.

If you insist on using a flash, use a diffuser. For a built-in flash you can tape a piece of white plastic garbage bag over your flash head or do something similar. (Tape the piece loosely and incompletely so that heat can dissipate.) For an external flash, you can buy a white plastic diffuser which fits over the flash head. However, you will find that even with a diffuser, a flash will still cause some glare. (Note that the point of using an umbrella is to diffuse the light and avoid the glare.)

When Do You See It?

With a flash, you don't see what you photograph until after you've taken the photograph. With umbrella lights, you see what you will photograph in your LCD window before you take the photograph.

Tripod

It's the mark of a serious photographer. It's not expensive. It's easy to use in a studio. It takes little expertise. And it's one of the best ways to increase picture quality. What is it? A tripod! Don't set up your studio without one.

Get a tripod with a good ball head. Ball heads are easier and more efficient to use than the traditional movable-plate heads. You can spend a fortune for just a ball head, but a $40 model is all you need. Some tripods in the $100-125 price range come with acceptable ball heads.

Figure 6.3 Manfrotto 724B lightweight tripod with ball head for digital cameras.

Efficient Workflow

It is difficult to take photographs that are so good that they don't have to have digital post processing. The old way—the chemical way—the processing was done by a photofinisher. Except for custom processing, photofinishers put photographs through an automatic process which improved them after developing and before printing. Without such processing, most prints looked rather dull. Today the process is digital, and you can do it yourself. Unfortunately, processing digital photographs can take as much time as you want to spend in an attempt to achieve perfection. The goal for eBay product photography is to spend as little time as possible and get good photographs.

The Basics

Before we get into the process, let's review the basics. Keep in mind that if you haven't learned shooting techniques and haven't devised a workflow for your digital photography, you may have to go to another resource (e.g., a digital photography book) to pick up that information before this chapter makes sense to you.

Studio

Photography is a serious business. You need to set aside some space for it. Let's call that space your studio. If you are photographing a variety of items, the space needs to be wider than a roll of background photographic paper and as tall as from floor to ceiling. For larger items you can use the floor. For smaller items you can use a table. And for even smaller items you can use the table and a matte board. Your umbrella lights will not take much space (folded) and can be set in a corner when you're not using them. A tripod can be folded and tucked away, if necessary. A 7-foot by 7-foot space may be all you need. Or, if all you photograph is small items, you can use a light box set on a table. You don't even need a tripod if the light box has built-in camera brackets.

Accounting

You need to devise a system to keep track of your photographs. If you take four photographs each working day for a year, you will have 1,040 photographs archived at the end of the year. That's a lot to keep track of. You need a file-naming system, an archiving album or storage place (software), and a means of posting the photographs to the Web. For items that you sell over and over again, you will want to make sure you reuse existing photographs rather than take new phtographs of the same items.

Software

You will need image-editing software to set up the processes covered by this chapter. There is so much competent image-editing software available that it would be a disservice to recommend any particular programs. However, I will mention that Adobe Photoshop Elements will be the featured software in *eBay Photography the Smart Way*. The reason for this is that Photoshop is the best image editor available at any price ($650 list price), and Photoshop Elements ($100 list price) has most of the functionality of Photoshop. Indeed, Elements is not only powerful software at a bargain price, but it's easy to use too.

A popular freeware program that has a lot of image editing power is Irfanview (*http://irfanview.com*). This might be a good starting place for you if you've never done any image editing.

Cropping

You want your item to fill the frame. This will make it as large as possible on a monitor screen. An item that takes up only a small portion of the frame may not show enough detail to be useful to potential buyers and in addition may look lonely.

This process can't be done automatically. You need to do it manually for each photograph. You can do it quickly, but it still takes time.

Brightness and Contrast

There are better, more advanced, and more efficient techniques for digital processing than adjusting brightness and contrast. But they are beyond the scope of this book. You can read about them in *eBay Photography the Smart Way*. In the meanwhile, adjusting the brightness and contrast can brighten up your photographs considerably.

For about 80 percent of my photographs, I decrease the brightness a little and boost the contrast. It brings out the richness in the color and makes the photograph more dazzling. Unfortunately, each photograph is different, and the other 20 percent require custom treatment. This process can be automated by batch processing.

Saturation

Saturation boosts the colors in a photograph. Usually just a little boost is good enough for most photographs, but some photographs require more than others. This process can also be automated by batch processing.

Resizing

You need to resize your eBay product photographs to the size they will be in your auction ads. About 400 pixels wide is optimal. You don't want your photographs to be so small they don't show any detail nor so large that they take a long time to download. Again, this is a process that you can automate with batch processing.

Sharpening

Sharpening should be the last step in the process. You want to sharpen exactly those photographs you will use in your auction ads. Sharpening unprocessed photographs or versions of photographs larger than those uploaded for eBay viewing does not work as well. Make sharpening the last step in the process after resizing.

Some photographs require more sharpening than others. Nonetheless, this process can be done automatically by batch processing with reasonable results. Keep in mind that you cannot sharpen a photograph that is out of focus.

Batch Processing

When you choose an image editor, you want to make sure it has a batch processing feature. This means that you can process multiple digital photographs (files) at once. As mentioned above, this will work for about 80 percent of the photographs you take under normal amateur shooting conditions. The good news is that product photography is normally done in a narrow range of shooting conditions (i.e., in your studio), and your percentage of uniform photographs will be higher. Therefore, batch processing may be effective for as high as 95 percent of your photographs.

Saving Time

Can you take photographs that require no processing? Sure. Many of the things covered by this chapter will help you do so.

Cropping When you take the photograph, fill the frame. You won't have to crop later.

Brightness and Contrast Take your photographs with soft diffused light. Experiment. As you get better at it, you won't necessarily have to correct your photographs in processing by adjusting the brightness and contrast.

Saturation This is like brightness and contrast. You may not need to adjust saturation if you learn to take photographs with soft diffused light.

Sharpening One of the great digital processing techniques is sharpening. Almost every photograph can use some. Nevertheless, if you make sure that your item is in focus when you shoot it, you can do without sharpening. If you can set the sharpening in your camera, set it to hard or maximum. You may not need to sharpen with your image editor.

Resizing Well, there's not much you can do about this. You will need to resize your photographs.

Alas, you can't eliminate resizing. But if you eliminate all the other processing steps by using diffused light, you will save a lot of time and effort.

Cost-Effectiveness Review

Good digital photography takes some time and a modest amount of money. Is it worth it? You bet! Taking good photographs is well worth it. It's important for boosting sales. It can make the difference between mediocre earnings and reasonable profitability. And it's essential to your success as an eBay retailer. For big ticket items, it's worth it to take great photographs. In so many words, attractive photographs are one of the most cost-effective things you can do for your eBay retail business whether via eBay auctions or eBay Stores. And Froogle also displays photographs.

III

Beyond the Basics

7

Data, the Key to Business Success

The digital age has arrived. Sooner or later you have to come to grips with it. eBay retailing is a digital business. It's tough to be successful without using auction-management software, image-editing software, and other key software aids that make an eBay retail business more efficient and more profitable. You don't need me to tell you that. What I'm here to tell you is that you need to understand databases too.

Now, I don't mean you need to learn database programming, create databases on your own, or become a database expert. That actually might be effort well spent, if you are interested in learning digital skills; but it's not necessary for success in ecommerce. What is essential is that you understand a few database concepts.

I have using computers for business since 1981, and I found a database important in the first year. In 1994, I put up my first ecommerce website. I did the catalog portion with a database. In 1995, I wrote a book entitled *Creating Cool Web Databases* (still in print) in which I explored how to create dynamic webpages with databases. (And I'm not a programmer.) In 1999, I wrote my first eBay book and devoted a considerable portion to using a database for eBay ecommerce management. Good software for managing eBay businesses had not yet emerged. Fortunately, the auction management services eventually relieved me of the necessity for that task and relieved you of wrestling with database programming too. Yet understanding databases is a recurring theme in the application of digital technology to business—including retail business.

At the Core

Auction management services have a built-in database at the core. For eBay, it's Turbo Lister. For Andale, it's Lister Pro. If you can understand database concepts, you can understand the vast potential for auction management services both today and in the future.

The *datafeed marketplace* is the most potent idea in this book. And how can you understand it without understanding some basic database concepts? You can't. So, here we go.

A database is simply a digital repository of data, a place where you store data in digital memory (e.g., on a hard drive). You create the data and enter it into the database.

A database needs a graphical interface in order for you to use it (unless you're a programmer. The form that this takes visually is a table. A table has rows (horizontal) and columns (vertical). You create the table and enter the data. For instance, you might create a table to keep track of your retail inventory. A row is a particular product. In each column, you store specific pieces of data about the product.

Records and Fields

Rows are also called *records*, and columns are also called *fields*. If you haven't heard of records and fields, don't worry about it. If you have used the terms records and fields, you will probably find it convenient to switch to using the more current terminology of rows and columns.

A retail inventory table (database – see Figure 7.1) might store information on a product that includes (Name – column name):

1. Product name   p_name

2. Wholesale price   w_price

3. Retail price   r_price

4. Number in stock   stock

Inventory : Table			
p_name	**w_price**	**r_price**	**stock**
FastFrames 14E	$231.47	$459.95	26
FastFrames 27H	$323.59	$595.95	4
FastFrames 409KT	$77.32	$119.95	37
FastFrames 723AR	$109.11	$169.95	9
FastFrames 45 Mark III	$51.72	$99.95	108
FastFrames 194XC	$542.29	$879.95	17
	$0.00	$0.00	0

Record: 14 ◀ [7   ] ▶ ▶l ▶* of 7

Figure 7.1 Database table.

As you can see in Figure 7.1, the product FastFrames 14E (camcorder) was acquired at a wholesale price of $231.47 and sells at your retail price of $459.95. You have 26 in stock. How did the data get there? You created the 4-column table with a database program (database manager) such as Microsoft Access. Then you entered the data about your inventory. For each product, you entered the pieces of data appropriate for each column. There you have it—a database full of data.

Data Basics

Databases are not difficult to understand. You start with the concept of a table as discussed above. Then, conceptually, you try to make the table(s) work for your business. This is a practical exercise, not a theoretical one. If the database is to be of value to you, you will be using it every day.

Design It

The first step in using a database is to decide what you want to keep track of. The following are good candidates:

- Inventory
- Auctions
- Buyers
- Transactions
- Fulfillment
- Follow-up

Then decide the data you will need to keep track of it. For instance, if you want to keep track of inventory, you might use a four-column database like the one in Figure 7.1. Envision it as a table. Rather than do a new example, let's look at the one in Figure 7.1 again, only this time in a Web browser (see Figure 7.2).

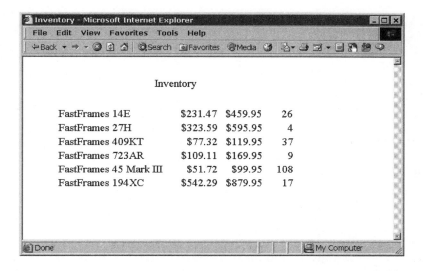

Figure 7.2 Simple database table displayed in Web browser.

Nothing is simple, however, and even for inventory control you will probably want your database to be more robust than just four columns. (This simple database is just for illustration.) Once you have set up a table, you are ready to enter data.

How Easy?

How easy is it to set up a table in software such as Microsoft Access or FileMaker Pro? Very easy. Not that I'm advocating that you do so. Leave your database work to the auction management service programmers. But if you had to do it yourself, it just isn't that difficult.

Enter Data

You can enter data into a database two ways. First, you can create a form with entry windows. A person can enter data in the form by typing the data in the entry window. This way is appropriate where the person entering the data is strictly a data-entry clerk. The data goes into the database table.

Second, you can enter data right into the table. This way is appropriate where the person entering the data has some knowledge about how databases work and is managing the database. For such a person, this way is easier and quicker. The person can enter data, change data, and otherwise manage data quickly. This is ideal for a small business, but the person must have some database-management skills.

Drudgery

Now it takes a lot of work to enter data into a database. It's drudgery. It's not the kind of work you want do (or pay to have done) any more than necessary.

Designing and creating the database itself can be fun. It's a high-level (easy) programming task that even non-programmers can do, at least for simple database applications. But you design and create the database just once (theoretically). Then you enter data everyday. Entering the data is the drudgery. And you want to make sure that in any database system (database application) that you create you don't have to enter the same data more than once. You might call it a *write-once* database system.

Get It All In

Now, you never want to put more data in a database than you think you will use. What's the point? On the other hand, you don't want to leave out any data that you think you will need. It's more trouble to go back and add a column to a database and then enter the data in that column than it is to do it right the first time. So, design your database to hold all the information you will need, and then enter all the data right from the beginning.

Take What You Need

Once you've entered all your data into your database, it's there when you need it. For any particular row (product), you can get all of the data or part of the data any time you want to. Let's say you expand your initial database design to look like this (Name – column name):

1. Product ID   id
2. Product name   p_name
3. Wholesale price   w_price
4. Retail price   r_price
5. Number in stock   stock
6. One-line description   one_descript
7. Marketing description   mkt_descript
8. Full description   full_descript
9. Initial bid   intial_bid
10. Reserve   reserve
11. Product photograph   p_image
12. Product URL   p_url
13. eBay category   e_cat
14. Froogle category   f_cat

When you want all or part of the data for a specific row (product), you ask the database to give it to you.

For instance, you can say to the database, Give me all the data for the FastFrames 14E row. And you will get all the data just for that product.

Or, you can say, Give me p_name, r_price, and mkt_descript for the FastFrames 14E row. And you will get the product name, the retail price, and the marketing description for that product, but nothing else.

Or, you might say, Give me p_name and r_price for all rows. And you will get the product name and retail price for all products.

Sound simple? It is. To manage a database, you have to be familar with the terms of database management, but those are not difficult to learn. For instance, you don't *ask* the database. You *query* it.

How Difficult?

How difficult is it to create queries? It's the most difficult task in database management. Why? Because the possibilities are endless, particularly in a table with many columns. Nonetheless, desktop database managers such as Access and FileMaker make it very easy to create a query.

Put It Together

Making data tables is not difficult. Entering data is not difficult. Asking the database for data (making queries) is a little harder but not difficult. This is simple stuff to understand, and it's relatively easy to make simple database applications. And even simple database applications can be very powerful.

Understanding data basics will go a long way toward understanding how database technology can help you in your business. And that means more sales.

Catalogs

What are catalogs? They're just templates with data in them. For instance, suppose you put FastFrames 14E in a page template with its product data and photograph. Then you put FastFrames 23M in another copy of the template with its product data and photograph.

You've just created two catalog pages. Suppose you use the same template for each. The catalog pages will have the same general appearance but will be different. They are different products with different product descriptions and different photographs.

Online

How do you sell merchandise online? You create a website catalog. What is a website catalog? It's a group of product webpages made from a template webpage.

If you don't want to create the template webpages yourself, what do you do? You obtain a program or a Web service that has created the template webpage for you. How do you use a template webpage? You enter your product data using one template webpage for each product.

Isn't every template webpage the same? Yes, it's the same before you use it. But it's unique after you enter the data.

eBay

The eBay template webpage is simply the eBay auction listing. Each listing looks the same but contains different data (see Figure 7.3).

Figure 7.3 eBay auction listing. ©2004 eBay Inc.

Froogle

The Froogle template is not a webpage. It's a section of the Froogle catalog webpage page. Each catalog webpage looks the same but contains different sections, each section representing a product sold by a different retailer. It is the data from each retailer that fills each section template of the Froogle webpage (see Figure 7.4).

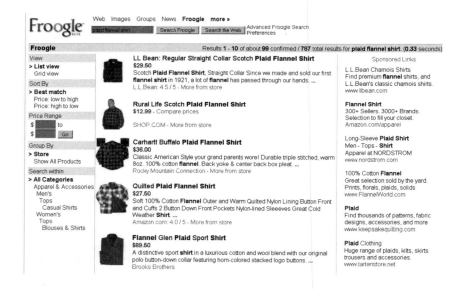

Figure 7.4 Froogle catalog webpage. ©2004 Google

It Uses the Data

A website catalog program or service is one that accepts data, places the data in a series of webpage templates to create the webpages that make up the catalog. And it does so quickly and automatically without any effort on your part.

Mail Merge

If you want to get a better idea of how you can merge data and a template to get a catalog page, read Chapter 17 about email marketing. It explains the mail-merge process. The process for creating Web catalog pages is the same.

Blossom

So, here's the story. The website catalog program or service is waiting for you (i.e., the template is waiting for you). You make a query to your database. The database program puts the requested data in a data file (a delimited text file). You export the data file from your database and upload it into the website catalog program or service. Where there was nothing before, suddenly a catalog blossoms. Depending on how much data you upload, the catalog might be 100 webpages or 10,000 webpages. A sudden blossom of 100 webpages is magic. A sudden blossom of 10,000 webpages is deep dark magic.

But let's get specific. You upload the proper data on 100 products to your eBay Store, and you suddenly have an eBay Store with 100 products listed in catalog pages, each on a separate webpage, where there was nothing before. You upload only that portion of your total data that eBay requires to make Store webpages. This is called a *subset* of your total data. The data subset is 100 rows containing the data below:

2. Product name	p_name
4. Retail price	r_price
6. One-line description	one_descript
8. Full description	full_descript
11. Product photograph	p_image
13. eBay category	e_cat

Note: These aren't all the columns you need to provide the data for an eBay Store catalog webpage, but you get the idea.

Again, let's get specific, this time about Froogle. You upload the proper data on 60 products to Froogle, and suddenly you have 60 product entries on Froogle webpages. You upload only that portion of your total data that Froogle requires to make catalog webpages. This is a subset of your total data. The data subset is 60 rows containing the data below:

2. Product name	p_name
4. Retail price	r_price
7. Marketing description	mkt_descript
11. Product photograph	p_image
12. Product URL	p_url
14. Froogle category	f_cat

And so it goes. For whatever catalog program or service you use, you query your database to create a subset data file, and you upload the subset of data required. A catalog then blossoms.

Files

What is a data file? It's simply a text file. It lists all the data pieces (column entries) defined by quotations marks and separated by commas or some other character. It's called a delimited file. If commas are used to separate the pieces of data, it's called a comma delimited data file. See a 3-row, 5-column comma delimited file below:

```
"id","p_name","w_price","r_price","stock"
"1409","Model 14E","31.47","59.95","26"
"1871","Model 23M","26.41","44.95","4"
"2302","Model 104FT","13.73","27.95","68"
```

Note that sometimes the column names are included in the database on the first line, and sometimes they are not.

After you make a query to your database, you can export the query as a delimited data file. By making the query, you create a subset of data. By exporting the query, you create a delimited data file. By uploading the delimited file, you provide the data to catalog software that the software needs to create catalog pages.

Different Catalogs

eBay Stores will require a certain subset of your data. Froogle will require a different subset of your data. Yahoo Shopping will require yet another subset of your data. And if you're operating an ecommerce website, the catalog program or service you use on your website will require still another subset of data.

So, you see, everything comes from your original database. Write once. That is, enter your data once. Publish everywhere. That is, use data subsets for multiple different catalogs.

What Database?

Do we recommend that you use an Access desktop database? Certainly not. Unless you're an expert computer user, you probably want something simple. It would be ideal to use software that did everything automatically for you—except enter the data.

Andale

That sounds like an auction management service such as Andale (*http://andale.com*). You can enter your product data into Andale's Lister Pro. Andale has built-in support for eBay auctions and eBay Stores. It also does a Froogle data feed (subset upload) and a Yahoo data feed (subset upload). It can even do a custom data subset upload suitable for a website catalog. In this case Andale's Lister Pro is the database.

eBay

eBay provides Turbo Lister, which is comparable to Andale's Lister Pro. In this case, Turbo Lister is the database.

Others

This is a very competitive field, and there are dozens of auction management services. You want to make sure you choose one that offers maximum flexibility. One of the programs (modules) in an auction management service is the built-in database. When evaluating auction management services, carefully consider what database functionality they each offer. The database functionality will be very valuable to you when you want to expand your sales to a marketplace such as Froogle.

Cost-Effectiveness Review

Databases are the backbone of most useful business software, and nothing in the history of retailing has done more to increase productivity than inexpensive access to the use of software. Enough said.

8

eBay Auctions and Stores

Let's take a close look at what eBay auctions and Stores do for you. They each do something different, and they complement each other. And they are both inexpensive compared to other online retailing opportunities.

eBay Auctions

eBay auctions enable you to sell items one at a time. Assuming you have different items, they will be spread all over eBay auctions into their requisite categories. As Gertrude Stein once said about an American city she considered boring, "There's no there there." Indeed, there is no sense that the eBay auction seller is a retail organization that exists someplace.

Because eBay auctions enables you to sell only one item per auction (or multiples of one item at one time), such auctions are not necessarily conducive to selling additional items to new buyers and existing customers. Consequently, it's up to you to do something to make your retail presence felt in eBay auctions.

Perhaps the best thing you can do is to run so many repeat auctions in the categories in which you sell products that it seems like you're always there. This gives the illusion of having a presence in eBay auctions. (But read the Volume Management section in Chapter 24 for the downside of such a practice.) Certainly this works for many kinds of businesses that make repeat sales of the same products day in and day out. Even those businesses, however, can get lost in pages and pages of items listed for sale on eBay auctions. If your strategy is to create a presence, you will do well to time your auctions so that they are spread over all of the listing pages of identical products being sold on eBay auctions. For instance, if you group them all together, they may appear on page 6 but on none of the other 14 pages of products eBay auctions generates for that type of product.

With this strategy you have to have your products spread out over the eBay auction pages day in and day out, 365 days a year, to maintain your presence in cyber world.

For those that don't have products that they sell each day repeatedly but rather sell only occasionally, this strategy doesn't work very well.

Another way you can enhance your marketing and establish something of a presence on eBay is to cross-sell. You can do this with a cross-selling device (panel) provided by eBay or another auction management services such as Andale. You can also do it by referring people to your other eBay auctions. eBay automatically lists all of your other auctions that you're currently running and will show such auctions if a buyer clicks on a link. This has some effect in establishing the illusion of your presence in eBay.

What is the great advantage of eBay auctions? The buyers are there. If you have the product, they have the money. A transaction is imminent.

eBay Stores

An eBay Store is different. It is a presence not only on eBay but also on the Web. It provides you with a permanent catalog of the products you sell. Unlike an eBay auction where you have to schedule your products and be careful how they are timed, with an eBay store you just put them in a catalog and they are available 24 hours a day for as long as you're willing to pay to have them there. Perhaps the prime difference between eBay auctions and eBay Stores is that everyone uses eBay auctions. Not so many people use eBay Stores. They are two different systems. When you look for products in eBay auctions you do not find products in eBay Stores (with some exceptions).

The reverse is not true. All of your current auctions are listed in your eBay Store. eBay Stores comprise a huge Web mall. Web malls have never been very popular. (Read more about Web malls in Chapter 24). Nonetheless, eBay Stores are becoming a popular Web mall for two reasons. First, they have the eBay brand which is very powerful. Second, you can use eBay auctions to market your eBay Store.

I would never advise anyone to operate an eBay Store without also putting products up for auction on eBay, too. Because eBay auctions are more popular than eBay Stores, you need to have a presence in eBay auctions in order to lure people to your eBay Store.

The question is, How do you do this? Well, eBay does something for you. It gives you a red tag icon in all of your auctions on which your buyers can click to go to your eBay Store. That's nice, but it's not enough. You need to continually direct people to your eBay Store from your eBay auctions. That means specifically putting links in your eBay auction ads which take people to your eBay Store. The link might read something like this, "Visit my eBay Store for a larger selection." So, it is quite clear to me that the way eBay auctions complement eBay Stores is through directing potential buyers to the latter.

The other question is, How do eBay Stores complement eBay auctions? The answer is simply that an eBay Store gives you a presence on the Web, a more concrete illusion of being an ongoing and responsible online retailer. It also provides you with opportunities to sell products to prospective buyers who are specifically looking for those types of products.

Unfortunately, eBay Stores don't work so well by themselves yet. Undoubtedly, someday eBay Stores will be as popular, or perhaps more popular, than eBay auctions. When that happens, it will be another reason for you to have an eBay Store.

The Datafeed Duo

eBay auction ads and eBay Store ads can come from the same database. Indeed, eBay's Turbo Lister or Andale's Lister Pro, typical listing databases, will send a datafeed to either eBay auctions or eBay Stores, or both. Consequently, in the world of datafeed marketplaces for eBay retail businesses, eBay auctions and eBay Stores are the first two datafeed marketplaces to which you will send your products.

An eBay Store as Your Website

An eBay Store gives you a unique URL (Web address) which, in effect, belongs to you as long as you maintain and pay for your Store on eBay. This is much easier and less expensive than establishing your own independent website. In addition, you have built-in eBay traffic which would take a huge amount of marketing (e.g., getting found by the search engines) on the Web to duplicate. In my opinion, most eBay retail businesses will not find establishing an independent website to be a cost-effective way of doing business on the Web. At least, not as long as they can have an eBay Store instead. An eBay Store gives you most of the good characteristics of a viable ecommerce storefront. It gives you a place, and more importantly, a place where there's traffic. It gives you a storefront look. It gives you a catalog of products. And it gives you a checkout mechanism. The checkout mechanism, of course, includes payment choices. You've got it all on with an eBay Store. Or do you?

The primary shortcoming of an eBay Store, as I see it, is the lack of capability to add content to your retail website. An eBay Store is pretty straightforward and does not provide you with the opportunity to add the kind of content you might add if you had an independent website. Content is a huge attractor which helps sell merchandise. Content also provides, or helps provide, great customer service. I see content as being an essential part of every retail business. In many cases, a business that cannot provide content on the Web is less than the best it can be.

Content

Content can consist of tutorials, reports, articles, checklists, and useful links. In short, content is useful information relevant to what you sell. See Chapter 22 for more on content as an attractor for retail businesses.

Even simple straightforward content such as how to use, clean, repair, and protect your products is better than nothing. Now to provide those four things on your website you may simply put links to a manufacturer's website. This does not mean that you have not provided content. Indeed, you have provided the content necessary to customer satisfaction just a click away. Customers certainly can't complain about that. What they can complain about is the lack of that information being readily available to them.

Some products are more complicated than others. For instance, if you sell chess sets, you may want to inform people how to care for them, clean them, and repair them when they get broken. This instruction will be straightforward and undoubtedly short. In other words, it's not a great deal of content. Nonetheless, it's content that helps customers use your products and shows them that you care.

On the other hand, if you sell radio-controlled self-powered model airplanes, there is a huge amount of basic information that you can give your customers on how to maintain and repair such a product. After all, it includes a high-tech radio controller and a motor as well as a fuselage with operational wings and stabilizers. Consequently, until eBay offers you substantial capability towards customizing your eBay Store into what will compare favorably with an independent website, you may have to resort to offering your content in a different place. Read more about this in Chapter 22.

Note that in both of the examples above, there is a second level of information that can be valuable to your customers and provide you with an opportunity to offer more content or even sell content. For example, chess players will want to learn how to play chess better. Give them a tutorial on playing chess or sell them a book on the same topic. Hobbists will want to learn how to control their model airplanes skillfully and put the planes through flying maneuvers. Give them a tutorial on flying or sell them a book on the same topic.

Cost-Effectiveness Review

Is it cost-effective to run eBay auctions? You bet! This is the heart and soul of your marketing effort. All of the other techniques in this book only complement eBay auctions. eBay auctions are ultimately cost-effective. But a word to the wise here. eBay auctions are only cost-effective if you use an auction management service. You cannot keep yourself well-enough organized to provide good customer service without the use of proper software.

Are eBay Stores cost-effective? A second, You bet! An eBay Store is inexpensive, similar to eBay auctions, handled by the same auction management service you use for eBay auctions, and provides a presence not only on eBay but on the Web too. As I hope I made clear in this chapter, however, you must use eBay auctions to drive traffic to your eBay Store to make it as successful as it can be.

The combination of eBay auctions and an eBay Stores is made even more cost-effective by the idea of the datafeed. Your products are in your database (e.g., Turbo Lister, Lister Pro). You can feed the data to eBay auctions and you can feed the data to an eBay Stores. Voila! Your products will magically appear in each place. Thus, the datafeed is the key to cost-effectiveness in jointly operating both eBay auctions and an eBay Store.

9

Creating Froogle Ads

OK, so you know how to do a datafeed. You're ready to go. This is quite exciting. By using a datafeed to create Froogle catalog product entries, you are expanding your market substantially. Read Chapter 2 and Chapter 7 to see how valuable this technique will be for increasing your revnue.

The real story here is not so much that Froogle can perhaps double your potential market. The real story here is that this is an incredibly cost-effective way to expand your market on the Web. Froogle was free in Beta and it's apparent since it's been out of Beta that Google is committed to keeping Froogle a marketplace that's free to retailers. Deals like this don't come along very often, and if you don't seriously consider doing a Froogle datafeed, you will miss out on a potentially substantial increase in your sales. Keep in mind the datafeed itself is simple, quick, and convenient if you use the right auction management service.

And now I want to raise a serious question. Several auction management services as well as eBay Stores claim that they do an automatic Froogle datafeed. If they do, is it effective? As you look at the criteria for the Froogle datafeed (see Details below), it makes you wonder. Without asking you to provide it, how do the auction management services and eBay Stores manage to get the specific columns (data) required by the Froogle datafeed? If you haven't input data specifically into such columns, either your auction management service or eBay Stores has to create the proper columns out of what you have input. And therein lies the mystery. What exactly do the auction management services do to in this regard?

Your concern here is that you get the full benefit of a competent Froogle datafeed, not a haphazard placement by a systemic scheme that may not work uniformly well for all retailers and all products. The devil is in the details, and you will want to know the details. Ask.

Executive Summary

What might be needed here is a new format for doing eBay ads. Instead of one space to put in your entire eBay ad, there should be two spaces. The second space would be for your entire eBay ad. The first space would be for an executive summary of your eBay ad. It would be the summary that would be transmitted with the datafeed to Froogle to become the description in the Froogle product catalog entry. (The description is allowed about 13,000 words, but Froogle includes only the first few dozen characters of the description.) With this kind of an arrangement, you would have total control over what happened on both eBay and Froogle. The executive summary would also be good for other datafeeds such as Yahoo Shopping or a comparison shopping directory.

An executive summary would also be good for eBay ads. An eBay ad should be long and contain a lot of product information, particualarly for expensive products or products with recurring sales. An executive summary at the top would serve the purpose of making it easy for prospective buyers to quickly decide whether the product was right for them. If so, they would go on to read the entire ad. If not, they would continue shopping.

Thus, if you provided an executive summary for an eBay ad, it would be helpful to eBay buyers and also serve as the description for the Froogle product entry. It would be in a separate column (in your database) from the eBay ad.

Because of the above considerations, I don't have full confidence in automatic datafeeds to Froogle and other datafeed marketplaces. Rather than have your auction management service or eBay Stores mishandle this process, you should be given the capability of creating your own Froogle datafeed and adding another column (field) in your database specifically to hold the Froogle description. This would enable you to do a custom datafeed. Of course, this means that you would have to take some action yourself using the requisite software procedures in order to do the datafeed. But better to do it right than to have some kind of a systemic scheme convenient to the vendors (and eBay) that doesn't do it properly.

Of course, if eBay Stores did provide for entering an executive summary, what I have said here would have less importance and urgency. So, stay aware of what's going on with datafeeds and lobby with both your auction management service and eBay Stores to establish a datafeed process that makes sense and works well to optimize your sales.

Use the Current Scheme

One way to use the existing scheme to your advantage is to start out (write) your auction ad with an executive summary, in effect. That executive summary might be two or three sentences—the first two or three sentences. These are the sentences that will appear in the Froogle catalog entry.

Although it's too early in the history of datafeeds to tell, it is my prediction that custom datafeeds, not automatic datafeeds, will be the most effective. For instance, suppose instead of providing an automatic datafeed, your auction management service enabled you to create additional columns in the listing database to provide precise Froogle datafeeds (and other datafeeds). And it also enabled you to do the Froogle datafeeds whenever you needed to. It seems to me that this would prove to be a more effective means of ensuring a high-quality Froogle retail presence than an automated scheme. But only time will tell how datafeeds will come to be used effectively. There is a lot to be said in favor of automation if it works.

More Than Data

There is more to datafeed marketing than just getting an item on a catalog webpage. Indeed, you may need to price the same item differently in different marketplaces. You also have to integrate the sales from each new datafeed marketplace into your retailing system and provide shopping carts, checkouts, and the like. That's where capable auction-management software can really prove its worth. Let the software handle these details. Otherwise, you will have to take the time to handle them.

Details

Below are the details of the Froogle datafeed. You will probably also need to read Chapter 7 unless you are knowledgeable in database concepts. A little bit of technical knowledge can go a long way toward understanding how digital schemes work and what the implications are for business.

The Data

The necessary Froogle datafeed columns are as follows:

```
product_url

name

description

price

image_url

category
```

Below are the explanations of each column (field):

Column 1: Contains the Web address (URL) of the webpage where the product is for sale.

Column 2: Contains the name of the product (up to 80 characters, same as an eBay title).

Column 3: Contains a description of the product (no HTML is permitted – up to 65,536 characters – about 13,000 words). Note that Froogle includes only the first few dozen characters of this description.

Column 4: Contains the price (fixed price required).

Column 5: Contains the URL of the product image.

Column 6: Contains the Froogle category in which the product is placed. There are also additional columns you can use if you need to run a more complex selling operation. You can find more details on the requirements at *https://www.google.com/froogle/merchants/ feed_instructions_new.html*.

Changes

Note that Froogle has made changes to its datafeed requirements in the past and presumably will do so in the future too. You need to refer to Froogle for the latest datafeed requirements, not this book.

The Froogle datafeed is a normal tab-delimited data file (database text file) that you can export from any database. First, you register your datafeed. Then you simply upload the file to Froogle, and that's your datafeed. Your auction management service should be able to do this effortlessly for a wide range of datafeed marketplaces including Froogle. If it doesn't, find another auction management service. If you need to engineer this datafeed yourself, Froogle provides detailed information on how to do so at the Froogle URL cited above.

For more information on datafeeds in ecommerce and for Froogle, look at some of the following resources:

CartKeeper, *http://www.cartkeeper.com/froogle.htm*

Subia, *http://www.subiainteractive.com/froogle.html*

K.Soft, *http://www.dummysoftware.com/froogie.html*

osCommerce, *http://www.oscommerce.com/community/contributions,2000/category,all/search,froogle*

SiteAll, *http://siteall.com*

Solid Cactus, *https://www.solidcactus.com/yadm/Default.aspx*

Always depend on Froogle itself, however, for the latest Froogle datafeed information.

The Business Requirements

Google doesn't let just anyone participate in Froogle. You must meet certain requirements. The requirements are mostly relevant to your merchandise, not to you. The following types of ecommerce websites are *not* permitted:

- Affiliates
- Multi-Level Marketing (MLM)
- Comparison Shopping
- Mirror

The following products are not permitted:

- Auction items, unless they have a fixed price
- Services or memberships
- Travel tickets
- Vacation packages
- Illegal products
- Products that include service agreements
- Customizable products without a fixed price
- Real estate
- Free products

If you are accepted to open a Froogle account, you may submit your datafeed as often as once a day and must submit it at least once a month to stay in the Froogle system. For current information, go to *https://www.google.com/froogle/merchants/policies_new.html*.

Results

You will want to observe the results in Froogle of any datafeed whether it be automatic or one that requires a custom set-up. It's the results that count. In other words, how do the product entries look? If an automatic Froogle datafeed gives you good results in Froogle, that's great. If it doesn't, you may find that a custom approach gets better resuts.

What are the desired results? As one well-known wag says, ninety percent of success is just showing up. If your Froogle product entry is complete and contains the requisite information and photograph, that's a good result. If it doesn't appear or if it's incomplete, that's a bad result.

Keep in mind that this is potentially a very important marketplace for you. You will want to monitor the results of your Froogle datafeed periodically to make sure it's working.

Quick Check

For a quick check of all your Froogle catalog entries, type the following into the Froogle search window on the Froogle webpage:

store:username

The user name is the one you register when you sign up to be a Froogle merchant.

Cost-Effectiveness Review

It doesn't get any better than this. This is one way to expand your sales in a grand way with little expense or effort. This is not something that you want to overlook. I could go on and on about Froogle, but the first two sentences say it all.

There's one caveat here. If your auction-management software cannot provide the processing infrastructure to handle sales in other marketplaces as it does for eBay, you may have to spend time managing the sales processes in such marketplaces. This could waste your time.

Let me just repeat that Chapters 2, The New Datafeed Marketplace, Chapter 7, Data, the Key to Business Success, Chapter 14, Developing a Datafeed Strategy, and Chapter 26, Analytics are the hard core of building your eBay traffic. If you do nothing else except what's in these chapters—plus provide good customer service—you will realize increased sales.

10

Creating Yahoo Ads

Yahoo Shopping is similar to Froogle. You just do a datafeed and your products magically appear in Yahoo Shopping as product catalog entries. What a deal! Unfortunately, as easy as this is to do, it's also expensive. Yahoo Shopping is going to charge you for every click-through. This charge seems small. If you assume that every click-through is a sale, the fees don't look like much. It's unlikely, however, that each click-through will be a sale. The ratio of click-throughs to sales will be different for different kinds of products, but it's likely to be high enough to become a major expense for selling your products.

Therefore, Yahoo Shopping is something to experiment with. It's not something to jump into with both feet and assume that you will have profitable retail sales.

Keep in mind that Yahoo has about 20 percent of the search engine market while Google has over 50 percent of the market. It seems likely that both Froogle and Yahoo Shopping will reflect the market shares of their parents. That is, Froogle will have about 50 percent of the market, and Yahoo Shopping will have about 20 percent. But the fact is that Yahoo Shopping charges click-through fees and is unlikely to get as many retailers.

The retailers that do sell through Yahoo Shopping are likely to charge more (i.e., pass along the cost of Yahoo click-through fees). You don't have to be a genius to figure out that it's unlikely that Yahoo Shopping will do as well as Froogle. Indeed, the Froogle market share may turn out to be above the market share of Google. A bigger marketplace attracts more potential buyers. More potential buyers create a better marketplace for online retailers.

Details

To do a Yahoo Shopping datafeed go to Yahoo Product Submit at *http://smallbusiness.yahoo.com/marketing/prodsubmit.php*. There is all the information you need to get started on Yahoo Shopping. The Yahoo datafeed is similar to Froogle.

Yahoo also provides storefronts (websites) for ecommerce, Yahoo Merchant Solutions (*http://smallbusiness.yahoo.com/merchant*). This is a popular hosting service. If you use a Yahoo storefront, you get a modest discount on Yahoo Shopping click-through fees. Although Yahoo Merchant is a significant marketplace, it doesn't seem to me to be a strong competitor to eBay. You are most likely better off with an eBay Store, particularly if you use eBay auctions to promote your eBay Store. It's certainly possible to have both an eBay Store and a Yahoo storefront just as it is to put your products on both Froogle and Yahoo Shopping. But is it worth the extra expense?

Note that Yahoo Merchant and Yahoo Shopping are separate systems, each with its own separate fees. Also note that Yahoo Merchant is a reasonable means of establishing a presense on the Web—probably preferrable to an independant website—if you choose not to use an eBay Store.

Cost-Effectiveness Review

Yahoo Shopping would be comparable to Froogle in cost-effectiveness were it not for the fact that it charges for each click-through. You will have to experiment with Yahoo Shopping to determine whether it's cost-effective for your retail business. It is important here to keep track of Froogle and Yahoo Shopping sales separately and do not mix them together. If you mix them together, it will be difficult to analyze whether Yahoo Shopping is worth the price of the click-throughs.

11

Creating Ads for Other Marketplaces

There are dozens of other datafeed marketplaces on the Web other than Froogle and Yahoo Shopping. On one hand, you can expect a big consolidation among the existing datafeed marketplaces. On the other hand, you can expect new datafeed marketplaces to pop up all over the place. Datafeed marketplaces are the latest killer ap in ecommerce.

If you're going to take advantage of datafeed marketplaces, you'll have to have software that will create the proper datafeeds. It would be nice if the datafeed requirements of other datafeed marketplaces were identical to Froogle. Then you could use the Froogle datafeed to put your products on the product catalog webpages of the other datafeed marketplaces quite easily. There will always be marketplaces that want to do things differently, though, and it would be nice to have the capability to create a datafeed that meets a variety of requirements.

You might ask yourself, Why would I want to bother with other datafeed marketplaces when Froogle is likely to expand my sales significantly more than any other marketplace? The answer is that every little bit helps. So long as every little bit doesn't cost too much money and it doesn't take much of your time or effort, it might be cost-effective and rewarding to expand into these other marketplaces.

This is true particularly when the marketplaces you want to use are specialty marketplaces. For instance, suppose you sell chess games, chess pieces, and chess paraphernalia. If someone creates a specialty datafeed marketplace for family games, that should prove to be an excellent place for you to sell chess sets. Therefore, you would want to send a datafeed to get into this specialty marketplace. If the datafeed required is different than Froogle, you'll have to create extra columns (fields) to enter the requisite data that goes into the product catalog entries for this particular marketplace. Your software will also have to have the capability to actually create and do a datafeed easily and quickly without any advanced high-tech knowledge and certainly without any knowledge of computer programming. Consequently, this is a feature to look for when you chose an auction management service to handle your eBay retail business. If you're already using an auction management service that does not provide this capability, demand it of your vendor and hope that you get it soon.

Again, some of the vendors will purport to do these datafeeds automatically to a variety of different datafeed marketplaces. The question you have to ask yourself is, How do they do this? This idea of using datafeeds to expand your marketplace is so new that it seems likely most of the vendors haven't rationalized their processes to the point where it makes it easy for you to take advantage of this new marketing technique. Make some noise.

Example Marketplaces

Chapter 2 provides list of datafeed marketplaces that you may want to investigate in order to supplement your eBay sales. Most are comparison shopping directories, which are currently very popular. They list products and provide a list of vendors and prices for each product. The vendors are rated by customers. The products are also rated by customers.

Most buyers use these marketplaces to find the lowest prices. They can look at the ratings of the various vendors and the rating of the product itself. Thus, they can find non-financial information upon which to make a decision as well as pricing information. Some datafeed marketplaces charge fees, and some don't.

Cost-Effectiveness Review

Again, the first question you will want to ask is, Does the datafeed marketplace in which I want to place my products charge a fee? If the answer is no, then it might be a good deal, particularly for specialized marketplaces where you can expect to generate some sales. If the datafeed marketplace charges a fee, then you have to look at the cost-effectiveness very closely and probably undergo some experimentation to determine whether it's worth it for you to sell there.

Specialized marketplaces might work well, and comparison shopping directories are quite popular. Check them out to determine whether they are cost-effective.

IV

Making It All Work

12

Auction Management Services

The auction management service is a great invention. I can't say too many times that you cannot achieve cost-effectiveness in your eBay retail business without the use of an auction management service. Whether you use eBay's auction management service or a third-party vendor's auction management service is not important. What's important is that you use some service to keep track of your eBay auctions and sales or else you will not be able to provide first-rate customer service and will likely go insane trying to hold your business together.

What is an auction management service? It can be software that you subscribe to, is delivered via the Web, and that you use through your Web browser. Or, it can be software that you load and use on your computer like any other program. Usually, it's a combination of the two.

Figure 12.1 Auction management services at Andale's website. ©2004 Andale Inc.

Some software vendors deliver more of their service via the Web and some deliver more of their service via programs resident on your computer. Either way, this book refers to auction management software as an auction management service.

Here are a list of things that an auction management service can do for you (based on a chapter in *eBay Business the Smart Way* Second Edition):

Inventory control

Presentation (templates)

Auction listings management

Customer communication

Auction follow-up

Checkout

Shipping

Transaction and fulfillment documentation

Feedback management

Sales Reporting

Accounting dovetail

Catalog

Datafeed

To do these things responsibly and effectively without an auction management service would take several employees. The cost of this type of service is low. It's extremely low when compared to having employees or independent contactors do it manually.

That doesn't mean that it doesn't require your time and effort or the time and effort of your employees to make it work. It just means that it cuts down considerably on the personnel requirement for getting the job done well. See *eBay Business the Smart Way* Second Edition for more about auction management services.

Datafeed Devices

Now and in the future one of the things you will want to look for in auction management services is the capability to do a custom datafeed. This requires two capabilities. First, you must be able to create extra columns (fields) to add new information to your database. The next datafeed marketplace in which you want to sell may require information (about products) that you've never entered into your database before. Second, you have to be able to assemble whatever columns you need to into a data set and export the data in such columns. When you export data, you are sending a datafeed. It is the sending of this data-feed which is the essence of datafeed marketing.

Datafeed marking caught on big time among auto dealers selling vehicles online in 2003-2004. The software designed for auto dealers to sell online contains the capability of providing datafeeds to various websites. There's even one service that offers to make datafeeds for datafeed marketplaces it does not yet serve. I don't see this capability available right now in most auction management services. But it does exist, and it will be widespread soon.

Here are a few of the auction management services offering datafeeds now (based on an incomplete survey at the eBay Live conference 2004):

Andale, *http://andale.com*

ChannelAdvisor Merchant, *http://www.channeladvisor.com*

Infopia, *http://infopia.com*

StoreFront, *http://storefront.com* (through a third-party add-on)

Truition, *http://truition.com*

Yukon Soft, *http://yukonsoft.com*

Zoovy, *http://zoovy.com*

(See *eBay Business the Smart Way* Second Edition for an extensive list of auction management services.)

As datafeeds are not considered serious selling features yet, it's difficult to obtain accurate information about what specific services are actually offered. Then too, the auction-management-service marketplace is changing so fast that information in books about software features is not likely to be up-to-date for long.

What Are They Doing Now?

Today many auction management services for eBay and eBay Stores claim to do a datafeed to Froogle. eBay Stores makes the same claim. That's primarily because Froogle is free. They can't automatically do a datafeed to Yahoo Shopping without your permission, because that would cost you money—unless they made their own special arrangements.

The question you have to ask is, How do they do that datafeed without its being set up properly? This issue is discussed in Chapter 9. To make a long story short, it may require an extra column (field) to do it right. There are other ways to do it effectively. But the person who does the eBay ad has to be involved in the overall process, it seems to me, in order for the content to be exported into Froogle rationally and effectively.

Datafeed capability is a process that is just beginning to be explored and established for eBay retailing. If the capability in your auction management service does not come quickly enough for you, squeal about it. It will come faster. The auction management service vendors not only need to provide this capability, but they need to provide it in a way that makes it easy and convenient for you to use it. You are the one that has to go out and find the appropriate and relevant datafeed marketplaces for your products. When you find them, it should be very easy to send the required datafeed.

Cost-Effectiveness Review

There are some eBay retail businesses that sell only a few products and nevertheless are profitable, even lucrative. For instance, if you are selling used airplanes at a minimum price of $165,000 each, you don't have to make very many sales each year to have a reasonable business. Your inventory may never exceed a three or four airplanes at a time. Your sales may not exceed one or two airplanes a month. And certainly you can keep track of such a sales program on paper without using any software.

Most businesses on eBay are not like this. To make a business profitable, particularly if it is a full-time business, you have to sell lots of products. To do it cost-effectively, you really don't have any choice except to use one of the very powerful and inexpensive auction management services that are currently available. This is a prime component in making an online retail business viable, whether it is on eBay or a part of any other online marketplace.

13

eCommerce Software

If you operate an independent website, you will need ecommerce software to sell anything on the website. eCommerce software consists of a product catalog, a shopping cart, and a checkout procedure. Also important is the capability to be able to use a credit-card charging service that dovetails with the checkout procedure.

eCommerce software varies in quality but is readily available from most host ISPs. In fact, host ISPs usually provide such software for a small fee or free as part of your website hosting service. Third-party software is also available.

One of the leading vendors is Miva, which provides Miva Merchant, an ecommerce software package. What's interesting and unique about Miva Merchant is that it accepts plug-in modules created by third-parties. The plug-in modules are simply additional software that extends what Miva Merchant can do. There a number of third-party vendors that create and sell Miva Merchant modules.

Miva Merchant by itself is a pretty capable ecommerce program, which runs on a Miva server. Miva servers are available at about 200 host ISPs. At a cost of about $700, plus yearly upgrades for $300 each, Miva Merchant is inexpensive for what it does. It's comparable to an enterprise program that provides a wide range of ecommerce services for a corporate website.

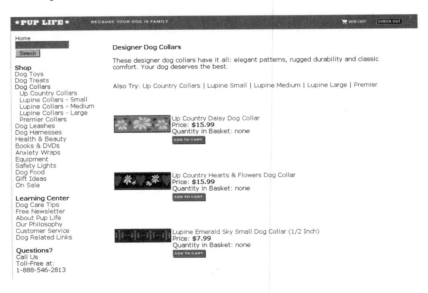

Figure 13.1 Pup Life's Miva Merchant catalog webpage.

With the additional plug-in modules available for Miva Merchant at low costs, you can turn Miva Merchant into a digital machine comparable to corporate software packages costing hundreds of thousands of dollars. For instance, there is a plug-in from Miva Merchant available for a modest price that will run an affiliate sales program for you. (See Chapter 24 for more information on affiliate programs.) This system provides you with a fabulous opportunity to use robust programming for increasing sales and delivering customer service that is otherwise not availabvle at an affordable price.

Independent Websites

eCommerce software is only important to you if you run an independent website where you sell products. Since this book does not advocate that you do that, I will not dwell upon the use of ecommerce software. However, what you should know is that the auction management services can provide many of the same features for independent websites. For instance, many auction management services provide catalogs, shopping carts, and checkout procedures that are essential to conducting business on the Web, and they are not necessarily confined just to handling eBay auctions and eBay Stores. They may also be used for independent websites.

The auction management services use an underlying database to provide services such as a catalog. Because they use a core database for their applications, they can do a datafeed. (Whether they enable you to do your own datafeed is another question, but they are certainly capable of doing a datafeed.) You can use their datafeed to populate a Miva Merchant catalog. In other words, if you have to use Miva Merchant at an independent website, it does not have to be an independent part of your retail operation. You can use a datafeed from your auction management service to put items in the Miva Merchant catalog just as easily as you can use a datafeed to put your items into the Froogle product catalog.

On the other hand, you can also purchase and install Miva Merchant modules into Miva Merchant that will keep track of eBay auctions and will do datafeeds to other marketplaces. It seems that the auction management services and the ecommerce programs are each coming from a different direction and meeting in a middle point somewhere where they start to look like one another.

The only thing you need to remember is that there are services and software that are very beneficial for you to use for a variety of tasks and a variety of online business configurations. It's up to you to choose your services or software carefully so that you are able to do whatever you need to do online without being restricted.

Cost-Effectiveness Review

I suppose if you have a large ecommerce website and your operations on eBay and eBay Stores are minor by comparison, that ecommerce software is important to make your business work efficiently. That's your most cost-effective approach. Be sure that you're using ecommerce software that provides the capability to handle eBay auctions, Stores, and datafeeds to other marketplaces.

If you are not already operating an online retailing business, I recommend that you use an eBay Store as a substitute for an independent website. An auction management service, whether provided by eBay or a third-party vendor, will provide all of the ecommerce functionality you will need to conduct your business professionally anywhere on the Web. Therefore, the message of this chapter is to use robust software to operate your business. But if you're an established eBay business thinking of expanding sales, don't worry about ecommerce software. You will be able to do almost everything just fine with an auction management service.

14

Developing a Datafeed Strategy

Chapters 2 and 7 explain the datafeed marketing concept. Now you've got to decide what you're going to do about it. You can't do everything—you can't be in every marketplace on the Web. But you can increase sales by expanding your offerings outside of eBay.

Datafeed Party

What's the best way to get started with your datafeed marketing? Have a datafeed party! What's a datafeed party? As first reported in *eBay Motors the Smart Way*, a datafeed party does not refer to a party with vodka on the rocks, Sushi snacks, and square-dancing music. It refers to the process of sitting down and researching how many places you can send data feeds to sell in new marketplaces. So, have yourself a datafeed party and see how many new marketplaces you can find to sell your [items] with little additional effort.

Since writing that for the *Motors* book, I have softened my hard-core position a little. Yes, it's OK to drink vodka and eat Sushi snacks during your datafeed party. But you get the point. Sit down and do some research on the Web to find some new marketplaces that you can use cost-effectively to increase your sales.

Used Cars

The used-car sales firms have utilized datafeeds very effectively to get their vehicles into multiple marketplaces (retail websites) on the Web. In fact, they are the leaders in using this new technique of datafeed marketing.

Procedure

When holding your datafeed party, here are some steps you need to take:

1. Identify datafeed opportunities by researching on the Web.

2. Determine the relevancy of the target website to what you are selling. For instance, if you sell perfume, a website that features a product comparison directory for scuba diving products may not be the best place for your merchandise, even if the datafeed is free.

3. Determine the market significance. Does the target website get substantial traffic?

4. Decide whether the marketplace a fit. The target website may be relevant with substantial traffic but still be a place where you

don't want to sell your products for one reason or another.

5. Determine set-up costs. Does your auction management service provide a datafeed to the target website, or will you have to arrange special programming?

6. Determine operational costs, including listing or click-through fees charged by the target website.

7. Identify what data you need to provide. Do you need to provide special data that you don't yet have in your database?

8. Figure out how will you will handle transactions. Do you have to do something special, or will your current capability (e.g., software) handle sales efficiently?

9. Review the cost-effectiveness of using the target website for selling your products.

Today there are many opportunities. Tomorrow there will be more. To operate cost-effectively, you will to be selective.

Why a Party?

Why make this research a one-time project? You will find doing this research in one sitting to be the most efficient. One link leads to another, and you can get a lot done in a morning or a day or a weekend. Doing it piecemeal is more difficult and tedious.

However, I don't want to leave you with the impression that once you're done, you don't have to do anything else. Periodically, you need to update your research to discover the new opportunities that inevitably appear.

Benefits and Burdens

What are the benefits and burdens of getting your products out into the general ecommerce marketplace (i.e., outside of eBay)?

- Potential to expand your sales cost-effectively

- Sell in a catalog format, not an auction format

- Sell in marketplace perhaps with less competition

- Sell in less complicated marketplaces (e.g., no non-paying-buyers and other complications)

- Tap into new markets with different types of consumers than the eBay market

There are also burdens to expanding sales into other marketplaces:

- Takes extra time to work other marketplaces even with the use of datafeeds available in auction management services

- Many datafeed marketplaces charge fees

- Different marketplace may have different transaction procedures requiring additional programming and supervision

- Makes invntory management more complex

Datafeed marketing presents a tremendous new opportunity for you. It's well worth doing. But you have to be intelligent in how you do it so as to minimize expenses and optimize profits.

Cost-Effectiveness Review

What does cost-effectiveness mean in regard to datafeeds? Well, there are only a few things to consider:

How much of your time will it take do the datafeed effectively? It could be as simple as clicking on a button in your auction management service. It could be as complex as setting up a datafeed procedure.

How much will it cost? Can you do do the datafeed yourself in a short time, or will you need to hire someone to set it up for you? How much money does it cost, if anything, to place your products on the target website?

What will it take to handle orders from other marketplaces? Can you do it with the software you are already using, or will it require something additional?

The datafeed itself is a software problem. It should be easy and inexpensive to conquer. Moreover, your auction management service should make datafeeds easy. If not, it may be time to move on to a more useful service.

The money question is straightforward. Is the datafeed presentation worth the fees charged? Like all advertising, only experimentation will tell. If the target website is free, the money cost is zero; although you will still want to look at the relevancy and traffic count.

Assuming the datafeed is easy, the target website has high traffic and is relevant, and the product listings are free (e.g., Froogle), a datafeed to a new marketplace can be one of the most cost-effective means of Web marketing. This is exciting not only because it is potentially quite inexpensive but also because it is new (i.e., undiscovered). This is a good place to focus your efforts to build your eBay traffic.

15

Developing a Multi-Domain Website

We all think of a website as being at one domain (website address). When you think about it however, there's no reason that a website can't span several domains. After all, how is a website held together? It's held together by hyperlinks (links). You click on a link in a website's home page and it takes you to another webpage on the website.

Some links in websites take you to a completely different website at a completely different domain (website address). Once you are at another website, though, there's no return to the first website. The sec-

119

ond domain, owned and operated by a different person or organization, will certainly have no return links to the first website.

But what if the second domain is owned and operated by the same owner-operator that operates the first domain. Then, the webpages at the second domain can look exactly like the ones at the first domain and, in fact, have links that return website visitors to the first domain. Therefore, if you control two domains (two websites, two web addresses), you can, in effect, make them into one website.

Website Visitors

What about your website visitors? Won't they think it's kind of strange when your webpages take them to URLs at a different domain? That's an interesting question. The fact is that the only way website visitors know that they're going to another domain is to read the Web address in the URL window near the top of the browser. Whoever does that? Indeed, it's unlikely that more than five people out of a thousand would notice the URLs of the webpages that they are visiting (except for the beginning URL). Thus, you can have a website that spans two domains without anyone perceiving that it spans two domains. If you can span two, why not more? Actually, you can span as many domains as you want and few people will ever notice. Of course, you must own and operate all the domains that you span and control the webpages and links at each website.

Servers

Why would anybody span two or more domains? Well, another host ISP may offer a service (usually delivered by a specialized server) that your current host ISP does not offer.

ColdFusion Server

For instance, suppose you want to create a Web-database application using Cold Fusion.

Cold Fusion

Cold Fusion is a Web-database application-development markup language that enables people who are not programmers to create Web-database applications using HTML-like mark-ups. If you know something about databases and can use HTML, you can use Cold Fusion to create powerful Web-database applications that otherwise only a database programmer would be able to create. To use Cold Fusion Web-database applications, your host ISP has to operate a Cold Fusion server. Without the server, your Cold Fusion Web-database applications will not work. There are hundreds of host ISPs that offer Cold Fusion servers to their clientele, but there are thousands of host ISPs that do not.

Your host ISP does not have a Cold Fusion server. You are happy with your current host ISP, which has been hosting your website competently, efficiently, and inexpensively for a number of years. Therefore, you want to find a second host ISP that does offer a Cold Fusion server in order to operate your Cold Fusion Web-database application. So, you register another domain and establish a second website with a second host ISP. There you can create webpages that include your Cold Fusion Web-database application. You span your website over both domains (over both host ISPs' servers) to create a unified website that very few people will ever notice uses different domains for different webpages.

Great Power

This has been a tiresome example. Nonetheless, it illustrates that the Web itself is a very flexible digital mechanism. What great power is at your fingertips!

If you can't do something you want to do at one host ISP, you can find another host ISP where you can do it. And your website can span both domains in such a way that no one is likely to notice. Each host ISP becomes a powerful building block.

Another Specialized Server

ColdFusion is just one example. There are hundreds of Web services requiring specialized servers that only a fraction of all the host ISPs provide. Any time you need to use one of these specialized services for some specialized device you are using in your website, you will have to use a host ISP that provides it. Your current ISP is not likely to be one that provides it. Thus, it's not uncommon for websites to span more than one domain. It's not a crazy as it sounds.

eBay

Have you ever noticed that eBay itself spans many domains? They are woven together seamlessly into one large coherent website.

Your Online Retail Business

Why in the world would you be interested in spanning more than one domain for your website? Let's take a look at why this could be valuable to you.

eBay Store

First, consider your eBay Store. It's where you have your ecommerce devices such as a product catalog and a check-out device. It has a unique URL that never changes so long as you maintain and pay for your eBay Store at eBay. Although technically it is not a separate website from eBay itself, as a practical matter it is a separate and unique website that belongs to you and over which you have control.

About Me

Then too, your About Me page has a unique URL that never changes so long as you are an eBay member. Although it is only one webpage, you can treat it like it is a website. There is no limit on how long the webpage can be, and you can put a lot of stuff on your About Me page that will help you in your retail business. You can consider your About Me page as a separate website owned, operated, and controlled by you, albeit it's only one webpage.

eBay Auctions

Your eBay auctions can each be considered a separate website, for the purposes of understanding a multi-URL website. However they are webpages that only exist temporarily. Typically, an eBay auction is up for a week or at most 10 days. Then it goes into the archives for three or four weeks, and then it disappears. While it's up, it has a unique URL and is controlled by you.

List of Auctions

There's one thing left out of this picture thus far. That's the eBay webpage that automatically lists all your current auctions. It's like a catalog in and of itself. And if you are to bring your three eBay websites together into one overall website, you will want to include this webpage (as a additional website).

Overall Website

A compelling idea is to create one website for your business that spans the "websites" as described above. That way, you can:

- Use your eBay auctions to promote your eBay Store, which is a very important marketing activity.

- Use your About Me webpage generally to promote your eBay retail business.

- Use your About Me webpage to publish short tutorials. However, there's some practical limit as to how much you can do on one webpage.

- Link to your eBay Store and to your About Me webpage from your eBay auction ads.

- Link to your eBay Store and to your eBay auction ads from your About Me webpage, although the auction links will constantly require new links for new auctions.

- Link to your About Me webpage from your eBay Store. eBay includes your auction ads in your eBay Store, so you don't have to make those links.

By linking back and forth, you can create the appearance of having one website and of having a presence on the Web.

The sky's the limit on what you can do here to pull all of your various eBay websites together into one overall website. If you do not have the understanding or competence with HTML that it takes to do this, take this idea to the person who does your webwork and discuss it with him or her. Pulling all these eBay elements together and using them to their maximum can create a more effective marketing machine for you than just using them the way that eBay has incorporated them into its overall system.

Portal Website

If you create an independent website, as Chapter 22 suggests, where you provide content as an attractor to generate greater sales, you will need to incorporate such a website into your overall eBay website. There are some serious barriers to doing this. For instance, eBay does not allow you to link to an independent website from an eBay auction ad. Likewise, eBay does not allow you to link to an independent website from an eBay Store webpage. Nonetheless, eBay does allow you to link to an independent website from your About Me page. Thus, if you are going to incorporate a Web portal into your overall multi-domain website, the linking will have to go through the About Me page. That's somewhat of a restriction, but it does not make the concept impossible. To give you a further understanding of how this might work, you need to know something about hyperlinks.

Types of Links

There are two kinds of Web links, external (to the outside) and internal (to the inside). We are all familiar with the external links that take us from one webpage to another webpage on the same website or to another website someplace else. What is not so obvious is that you can create a link in a webpage, not to another website or another webpage, but to another place on the same webpage. By using a combination of external and internal links, you can be very creative in building a multi-domain website.

Links to the Outside

Suppose you are viewing the webpage *http://chessfun.com/moves/first.html*. An HTML link to a place outside the webpage might look like this:

<a src="http://chessfun.com/moves/advanced.html">text</a>

<a src="http://familygames.com/chess/pieces.html">text</a>

In the former case, the link goes to another webpage on the same website. In the latter case, the link goes to another webpage on a different website.

Links to the Inside

To create an inside link, first you need to create an anchor. Each anchor has a unique name inside the webpage. Anchors look like this when you see the HTML (but are invisible to webpage visitors):

<a name="king">

<a name="queen">

<a name="knight">

Once you have created anchors, you can link to them from inside the same page. Suppose you are viewing the webpage *http://chessfun.com/moves/first.html,* and it includes the three anchors above. A link in the webpage will take you right to one of the anchors:

> *<a src="#knight">* text *</a>*

Once you have created anchors, you can link to them from the outside too, that is, from another webpage. Suppose you are viewing the webpage *http://familygames.com/chess/moves/novice.html.* It can include a link to the anchor named *knight* in the webpage *http://chessfun.com/moves/first.html.* The link looks like this:

> *<a src="http://chessfun.com/moves/first.html#knight">* text *</a>*

HTML is a slick system with a lot of flexibility. That's why a working knowledge of HTML will help you understand the possibilities even if you don't actually create webpages yourself.

Navigation Menu in About Me

This is an example of something you can do with your About Me webpage. Suppose you have an independent website where you feature content (attractors) to help generate additional sales. The home page at this website has a navigation menu. Let's call it the Content Navigation Menu.

Next, suppose you create an anchor named *menu* someplace in your eBay About Me webpage. Just below that anchor you place a duplicate of the Content Navigation Menu.

Now you can have a link in an eBay auction ad or an eBay Store catalog webpage that goes directly the Content Navigation Menu (for your independent website). And it doesn't violate eBay rules because the link actually goes to an anchor in your About Me page.

This is one illustration of how you can tie together multiple domains (websites) into one overall website.

Making It Work

How do you make all this work? The diagram below (see Figure 15.1) will give you a start on understanding how to make this all work and why it could be important to your marketing effort, that is, building your eBay traffic.

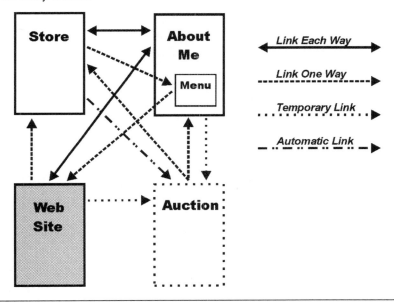

Figure 15.1 Overall eBay website.

All the Tricks

eBay can't anticipate all the tricks that webmasters will use to get around its rules. Consequently, it changes the rules periodically to plug up the work-arounds (loopholes) that webmasters create. You may find the work-around in this section to be outlawed by eBay someday. If so, it's time to create another work-around.

In this case, eBay has no gripe. You're just providing content (attractors) on your independent website, not making sales. But often an eBay rule intended to prevent the avoidance of eBay fees can prevent legitimate online activities.

Cost-Effectiveness Review

To use this marketing technique effectively, you have to be able to create your own webpages. That is, you have to understand how to use HTML. If you don't, you'll have to pay a webmaster or Web developer to do this for you. Consequently, this can be very cost-effective if you have HTML skills, and it is perhaps less cost-effective if you have to hire somebody to do the work.

The real question is, What's the priority for creating an overall website for your eBay retail business that spans even to an independent website? I consider this a very high priority. It's a high priority because eBay Stores do not yet have the massive retail attraction that eBay auctions do. Consequently, it is necessary for you to use eBay auctions to promote your eBay Store. Use your eBay auctions to take people to your eBay Store. Include text in your eBay auction ads that inform website visitors to visit your eBay Store and include links in such text. For this reason alone, it's important for you to consider the spanning ideas presented in this chapter.

Whether it's cost-effective to integrate a portal into your overall eBay website depends on whether the portal itself is cost-effective (see Chapter 22). If creating a portal is cost-effective and if optimizing it for the search engines is cost-effective , then it is absolutely cost-effective to incorporate it into your overall eBay website by using links from your About Me page. Perhaps one of these days, eBay will recognize the importance of having an independent website that does not sell products but rather provides content and will allow such a website to be linked driectly from your eBay auction ads and your eBay Store catalog webpages.

V

Special Techniques

16

Getting Found by the Search Engines

Getting found by the search engines has been the traditional way of selling products on the Web. It has been essential to online retailing. With the advent of eBay's rise to prominence, however, getting found by the search engines is no longer the only road to online retailing success. eBay Stores combined with eBay auctions now presents a lower-cost alternative. Nonetheless, it is worth taking a look at website optimization to understand the alternatives.

Website Optimization

Website optimization is the process of creating webpages that get a high ranking in the search engines. What does this mean? This means that you want the home page of your website to not only be found by the search engines but to be listed by the search engines in the first page of returns. Even being listed on the second or third page—a lower ranking—is probably OK, but certainly not ideal. Beyond the third page, your business might as well be invisible. Thus, a high ranking is essential to online retailing success. And website optimization becomes the name of the game.

Unfortunately, the optimization process is not only for the home page but for all the other important pages on your independent website. If you are selling many products, at least the important pages that head product categories need to be optimized.

Cost

The cost of optimization is high. The cost depends on the niche, the amount of competition in the niche, and the character of the domain name. It can take anywhere from a few days to a few weeks of labor by both you and your optimization consultant—most likely the latter. A typical optimization fee for an independent consultant might be $6,000—less for a narrow niche with little competition and more for a wide niche with plenty of competition. Then there is the follow-up task of ongoing optimization which will cost an additional amount. If you have the optimization done by a consulting firm instead of an independent consultant, it will cost even more.

Unfortunately, in the website optimization business, there are a lot of con artists. They promise to get your website found by the search engines for a one-time registration fee of $50, $500, or $1,500. Optimization is expensive, and you need to beware of consultants (vendors) that offer to do it for you on the cheap.

One way to beat the high front-end cost is to engage a vendor that does it for a high monthly fee. A $1,500 to $2,000 per month fee is typical for professional optimization services. A one-year or two-year contract is normally required.

In addition to the amount you have to pay a vendor, it will require a great deal of work on your part (or by your webmaster). Only you know your business and website well, and a vendor will work with you to create the webpages necessary to optimize your website. If the website optimization vendor does not require you to do a lot of work—and help you to do such work—you will probably find that you are not getting competent assistance.

It's Not the Fees

Obviously, it's not the fees that determine the competence of an optimization consultant. Good consultants (good firms) charge healthy fees. But bad consultants can charge high fees too. So, choose an optimization consultant carefully.

eBay Stores

eBay is a terrific brand name for selling at retail on the Web. It draws millions of potential buyers. By establishing an eBay Store instead of an independent website, you take advantage of the eBay brand and do not have to worry about website optimization for the search engines. If the traffic generated by eBay stores is not enough for you—and it probably won't be—you can use eBay auctions to promote your Store, thereby creating additional traffic for your Store.

eBay has a close relationship with Google and spends plenty of money promoting and advertising on Google. Thus, by virtue of having an eBay Store—and even using eBay auctions—you will get traffic from Google, the Web's leading search engine. It seems, therefore, that for many small businesses, there's no longer any reason to have an independent website to sell products.

Datafeed

Google has created Froogle as its retail search engine. You use a datafeed to make Froogle work for you (see Chapters 9 and 14), not optimization. And the datafeed is free. Thus, optimization for Google becomes even less important, and maintaining your datafeed becomes crucial.

Portals

If you operate a Web portal as suggested in Chapter 22, you will have reason to optimize this portal. Although you don't need to optimize it for customer service—you can direct your customers to the website where you provide customer service—you will need optimization to make your content (attractors) work. The tutorials, articles, checklists and other informational content that constitute your attractors are not likely to be found by people unless the attractor webpages are optimized for the search engines.

Since many attractors are also customer-service devices as well, attracting the general public may not matter to you. That is, your purpose may not be to generate additional traffic. But if your purpose in putting up the attractors is to generate additional traffic to your eBay Store—via your independent website as explained in Chapter 15— you will need optimization.

Unfortunately, optimization for an independent website is an expense you're not likely to be able to afford until your business has become profitable enough to carry on expensive advertising and promotional campaigns. Hence, the good news is that you don't have to have an independent website to be a successful online retailer today; but the bad news is that if you want to use a portal with attractors to generate additional traffic for an eBay Store, you'll have to spend the money and put in the effort to optimize your portal.

Search Engines

For which search engines do you need to optimize your website? Google has over a 50-percent share of the search-engine market. Yahoo, second-place runner up, has about a 20-percent share of the search-engine market. That means between the two of them they generate 70 percent of searches on the Web. This shows that when you optimize your website for the search engines, the only important search engines are the top half-dozen. Beyond that your time, effort, and money will earn quickly diminishing returns.

Regretably, maximizing for Google is different than maximizing for Yahoo. One of the things a good optimization consultant can do for you is to help you create webpages that will optimize your website with both search engines and perhaps three or four more at the same time.

Then too, there may be specialty search engines that are particularly important to your business. For instance, if you sell gourmet food, there may be a search engine that specializes in helping people find gourmet food websites. It would be worthwhile to make sure that your webpages were optimized for such a specialty search engine. But that would be the exception to the rule. The rule is that it is only worth your effort to optimize for the top half-dozen search engines that have the top half-dozen market shares.

Cat and Mouse

The search engines endeavor to help people find exactly what they are looking for without any outside influence. Web retailers seek to influence the search engines to give their webpages priority. The retailers and the search engines have played this cat-and-mouse game since search engines first appeared on the Web in the early 1990s. It is a very complex cat-and-mouse game, and the rules change every day. Website-optimization consultants tend to be smart people who work hard at keeping up with the latest changes, rules, and algorithms used by the leading search engines. That's why optimization is expensive. And that's why those who claim to do it for small fees—and without much work on your part—are likely to be scammers.

An Alternative

An alternative idea to that expressed in this chapter is to forgo using eBay and eBay Stores and just use Google (Froogle) and Yahoo (Yahoo Shopping). Naturally, this would require an independent website. The most effective way to make this work, however, doesn't have to be optimization; instead, it can be advertising. You can buy keyword ads on Google—ads that appear only when certain keywords are used to make the search—and place products in the product comparison directories, which are growing quickly in popularity. In other words, you don't ever have to optimize.

This works best for successful businesses with substantial advertsing budgets that list products in large volumes. You will save a lot of money on eBay fees, but the savings have to be enough to pay for the advertising and the fees for placement in the product comparison directories.

Cost-Effectiveness Review

At one time website optimization was the only dependable Web marketing technique. Sure, online advertising and offline advertising drove traffic to a website too. But that approach was usually more expensive than optimization. Consequently, optimization was considered to be a cost-effective means of creating adequate retail traffic to run a business.

Fortunately, eBay auctions and eBay Stores have created a retail environment which no longer requires you to spend money on website optimization (or advertising). For this reason, optimization must now be considered less cost-effective than it used to be. I do not recommend that you have an independent website specifically for selling products, and therefore I cannot recommend optimization as a means of driving traffic to such a website. Nonetheless, there are several considerations to keep in mind.

First, if you are operating an independent website where you sell products successfully and are using optimization to do so, keep on doing it. If it ain't broke, don't fix it, as the wags say.

Second, if you decide to operate a Web portal with content that includes attractors to generate traffic for your retail business, optimizing such a website for the search engines is something that you will probably need to do. But such an approach to generating more traffic is available only to eBay retail businesses that can support an expensive marketing campaign.

Third, there will always be businesses that will be exceptions to any rule. In this case, retail businesses with high listing volumes may find that using Google (Froogle) advertising and placing products in the leading product-comparison directories will incur lower costs and will still achieve success. They will do this by not bearing the expense of using eBay auctions, eBay Stores, or optimization .

17

Email Marketing

With email you can carry out a variety of marketing campaigns. These are effective campaigns that you do with a minimum of time, effort, and expense. If you're not emailing already, you're missing out.

Chapter 3 on customer service covers using an email follow-up system for buyers. Therefore, I won't cover that important and necessary process here. But that leaves you plenty more to do with this versatile communications device.

Email Techniques

Let's look at a few things you can do with email. This is not a complete list, but it will get your imagination stirring.

Spam

Spam is unsolicited email to a general mailing list (purchased). There are thousands of general mailing lists around, some with staggering numbers. For instance, it's not uncommon for someone to offer to sell you a emailing list with 10 million names. You need only a minute return on spam solicitiations to make significant sales. For instance, a .01 percent return (one one-hundreth of one percent) on a mailing list of one million is 100 sales. Consequently, spam has an unholy attraction to many retailers.

I don't recommend spam. There's too much of it already—obvious to say—and it's likely to become less and less effective. It won't enhance your reputation. It requires special techniques to avoid being blocked by multiple Internet service providers (ISPs). It is blocked by anti-spam systems and software. It's illegal in some forms and in some places. It's likely to be illegal in more forms and more places in the future. And there's a certain ethic that requires us to all participate in the effort to keep the Internet an efficient means of communications. Spam horribly violates that effort.

Nonetheless, there are other methods similar to spam, which are perfectly legitimate.

Opt-In Email

Some of the same vendors that offer general emailing lists also offer so-called "opt-in" emailing lists. Let's say you go to a retailer's website to buy perfume. You buy a $60 bottle of some odoriferous liquid. When you go through the check out, there's a sentence with a box after it. The box is conveniently checked for you. The sentence is:

Yes, I would like to receive information on other fragrances.

If you do nothing, you have opted into a mailing list. You have to uncheck the box to keep your name off the mailing list.

According to the way the sentence is worded, you would expect to be emailed only about other purfumes that the retailer sells. But that might be a false assumption. First, the retailer might very well send you emails on cosmetics or even designer clothing. Second, the retailer might sell its mailing list, and then you might get email from another retailer in regard to purfume, or cosmetics, or whatever—supposedly something at least vaguely related to purfume.

In other words, the people on an opt-in mailing list supposedly have some interest in the type of products for which they opted in. How intense that interest might be is another question.

Buying an Opt-In List

If you buy an opt-in mailing list, you will want to make sure that the type of products opted for are close to what you're selling. An opt-in mailing list can be so vague that it's practically a spam list. However, an opt-in list assembled for products that are identical or similar to yours can be worthwhile. The receipients presumably will be interested in what you have to sell.

With an opt-in list, you match the advertising to people's interests. This type of emailing is not spam because it is solicited from website visitors. The solicitation may be weak or strong, auctual or implied, but there is some relationship—however tenuous—between the prospective customer and the products offered. Let's call this type of emailing *direct email* to differentiate it from spam.

The Best Opt-In List

The best opt-in eamiling list is the one derived from your list of customers, past and present. It is implied that your customers will be interested in anything you send them. After all, they've already paid you for merchandise. A direct emailing to a purchased opt-in mailing list might work well, but an emailing to your own customers has to be the ultimate in direct emailing; this is, the ultimate in effectiveness.

Direct Email

What does direct email look like? Well, it's very likely to be personalized. That is, the receipient's name and other tailored information—from your database—will appear in the body of the email message. (Read below about mail merging to see how to do this.) In addition, you will want to give every receipient an opt-out (unsubscribe), an election not to receive future direct emails.

Other Direct Solititations

You could add to your direct emailing list by contacting eBay bidders on products similar to the ones you are selling and somehow get these bidders' email addresses. That is clearly in violation of eBay rules if you use addresses to do emailings that attempt to undermine other sellers' auctions or avoid eBay fees. It's not so clear that it's a violation if you solicit such prospective buyers well after the auction is over with a routine emailing. However, in that case it would be spam, which is also an eBay rules violation.

Is it a violation of eBay rules if you send direct email to eBay members who have bid on your products but have not won the bidding? You will want to check the eBay rules carefully—keeping in mind that they change often—before doing any emailing beyond your own customers.

What is clear is that you can use direct email with your own customers (winning bidders), at least until they opt out.

The remainder of this section indicates some of the forms direct email might take.

Cross-Promotion

Because you know what your customers have purchased, you can cross-promote accessories and related products. See Chapter 19 for more information. In other words, if someone purchases perfume, send them a direct email that sells them some cologne. The mail-merge in this case would be only for those of your customers who bought perfume. Or, since perfume is related to cosmetics, you might do a cross-promotion for cosmetic products.

Survey

A good way to get marketing information is to ask for it. To do this you might run a survey by direct email. Your returns won't be high, but you may get some useful information. If you want your returns to be higher, offer something enticing to the receipents (e.g., coupon for a 10-percent discount).

Transportation

Don't forget that email has the powerful capability of transporting other digital devices. It might be a digital photograph, an audio bite, a video clip, a text document, a multimedia document such as a webpage (i.e., HTML email), a program, or almost anything. This gives you a lot of versatility.

Support

You can provide support for your products by email. You don't want to jump into this without thinking it through. For instance, suppose you sell DVD drives for PCs at commodity prices. Support for this product could be a high-tech nightmare. And the buyer doesn't expect it. There are thousands of PC consultants and PC maintenance people who provide support services. And most manufacturers provide support too. Support is not expected from a retailer who sells at low prices.

But, suppose you sell voice recorders for dictation. These are sophisticated devices often complicated to operate. A beginner may have trouble using one. Where does she go to get help? There are not many places. Most likely she will look to you for support. And email can be a cost-effective means of providing it.

Newsletter

Do a newsletter and send it via email. If you want to be fancy, send an HTML email newsletter. Or, if you want to be extra fancy, send a nicely typeset PDF newsletter that readers will be likely to print on their computer printers.

Newsletters make a great marketing device. You can make them do almost anything you desire. They can provide information on how to clean or repair products, on new products in the pipeline, on multiple uses for products, on closeouts of products, on accessories, on personnel in your business. etc. The list is endless.

Resources

There are dozens of email-management programs. Some provide the basics. Some provide comprehensive functionality. Try these:

ConstantComment, *http://roving.com*

Topica, *http://topica.com*

WorldCast, *http://fairlogic.com*

Keep in mind too, that many auction management services provide email management software.

It's the Database...

It could be said to remind us of what's important in marketing that, "It's the database STUPID." However, we'll leave that kind of talk to certain other eBay books. Here we'll stay Smart, and just say, "Even for email, remember the database."

Your Database

Your database has substantial information on each of your customers. Name, address, phone number, email address, items purchased, and other data. You can use this data to customize your email for each recipient.

Mail Merge

You customize by mail merging. This is the digital process of merging data into form letters (i.e., form email messages).

Take the Data

You export the data from your database in a delimited text file. It is now ready to be used by a word processor or email program to merge into individual custom letters or email messages.

Take the Email

Before you can mail-merge, you need to create a template letter or template email message. In the template are certain codes that designate where certain data will be merged into the letter or email message.

Merge and Send

Microsoft Word has robust mail-merge capability and can do your mail merge quickly with a high degree of automation. There are also email programs designed to do mail merging. Such programs usually include a mail server so that you don't have to send the mail through your host ISP. (Some host ISPs put a limit on the amount of email you can send as a means of preventing spam.) One example is Fairlogic's WorldCast (*http://fairlogic.com*).

The mail-merge function takes the template and merges selected data from one row (record) of data into the template, prints it or sends it, and then repeats for the next row. Thus, it creates a succession of custom letters or email messages.

Mail merging is easy to do and works very well. It's the initial set-up that requires a little work. After that, mail merging runs practically automatically.

Not Just Words

You can mail merge more than words. You can merge phrases, sentences, paragraphs, HTML mark-ups, and other text into a template. For instance, if you have the URL of an image (and the HTML image mark-up) in a database, you can merge that into an HTML template, and the image will appear in the resulting webpage or HTML email.

Auction Management Services

You don't need Microsoft Word or WorldCast to do a mailmerge. Other programs can also have built-in mail-merge functionality. When you select an auction management service, you will want to make sure that it can mail merge. If it can, the mail-merge process is likely to be highly automated.

Custom Communications

Mail merging is wonderful. It enables you to send custom communications to your customers, enabling such systems as customized cross-promotions and customized customer service. Whether it's a webpage or an email message, customization works well for marketing.

eBay Auction Ad

An eBay auction ad is the result of a mail-merged webpage template. You submit your data on auctioning an item to eBay. eBay keeps it in a database. When a website visitor clicks on your title in a listing page of titles, the eBay Web-database application takes the auction-ad template and the data for your listing and mail-merges it into the auction-ad webpage. The auction-ad webpage is said to be created on the fly since it didn't exist before the merge.

Cost-Effectiveness Review

Email is a powerful and cost-effective tool to use for marketing. The more automated your mail-merge system, the more cost-effective your emailing campaign. And remember, it's a customized marketing campaign.

18

Marketing in Communities

Community is touted as a great way to market products and services. Is it? Well, it's a mixed bag. First take a look at what community is before you decide whether it's right for you and your products.

Community is any device online where people of like interest come together online to communicate. Community can be an online forum where members of the forum group send messages to the group at their convenience (not in real time). These are called Discussion Boards by eBay. They are also known on the Internet as listservs, forums, discussion groups, or blogs. Community can also be an online chat group where group members talk with each other, in effect, in real time. The talk is text that's typed on a chat screen. Chat can be messaging (e.g., AOL Instant Messaging) when it is not open to the public and controlled by each user. Forums and chat groups have differences in regard to the cost-effectiveness of your online marketing.

From your point of view, you can be a participant in a community or a sponsor of a community. Each is a different roll and each is different in regard to the cost-effectiveness of your marketing effort.

Internet Programs

There is a variety of software that supports online communities. Some of it is available from your host ISP (usually at no extra charge). Some you can buy and load on your host ISP's server as a CGI script (not difficult to do, but not a task for novice computer users either). Some of it is provided by special vendors and works on special servers on the Internet (an easy means of use), which you link to from your website. To understand what the software does and how to use it, you have to pay careful attention to the particular software product.

Forums

Forums use email messages to communicate, but not in real time. Participants send a message to the forum, and the forum receives the message and sends it to all forum participants (members).

A listserv is a good example of a program that does this. It works strictly with members' existing email programs. It's up to the member to arrange and keep track of the emails he or she receives from the listserv.

There are also Web forum programs. eBay's Discussion Forums are a good example. You use something that looks like an email program to send messages, but the interface is inside your Web browser. You also look at the messages with your browser that other members have sent.

The messages are in archives on the forum website and usually arranged in *threads* according to the topic discussed.

Since you send messages or read them at your convenience, the conversation that takes place through the forum is said to be not in real time.

Chat

Chat takes place in real time. To take part in chat, you have to be online at the same time as the other members. It is like an ongoing conversation, but it is with writings, not sounds. There dozens of different chat programs that each work a little differently. Chat programs are hosted by someone but opened to the public—or perhaps open only to those with password access.

Messaging is typically a system sponsored by a large entity. AOL Instant Messaging is a good example. Each participant configures his or her messenger program to include or exclude other people. So messaging is not necessarily public, but it can be. It's a way to talk with only the people you want to talk with.

Blogs

Blogs are the latest Internet phenomenon. They are essentially a bulletin board where the blog owner posts his or her writings. Blog members can read the writings but cannot respond publically on the bulletin board. They can respond privately to the blog owner. And the blog owner can reveal publically communications from whomever.

If you operate a blog, you will want to keep professional. Discuss only matters that relate to your products or the industry the products represent.

Many blogs are personal diaries. Make sure your blog isn't one. If you want to flaunt your personal life before the public, do it far far away from your eBay retail business.

Passive Participation

Passive participation is not what this chapter is about. Passive participation is simply viewing a forum routinely, or occasionally, and observing what people are saying without making a contribution yourself. Let's analyze this.

Passive participation is not a marketing program, because you have no visibility. So what is it? And how can it help your marketing? Well, it is a source of information. It is a jumbled mass of information, to be sure. Still, it can be a very valuable source of information.

If the topic of the forum fits your products, the forum may be a great place to get consumer input. Listen to what the consumers are saying about products. Then too, the forum might be a place to learn about your products from others who know more than you know. Finally, the forum might be a place for you to ask questions about products occasionally and get useful answers. This passive participation may well help you in your marketing efforts, but it is not itself marketing.

Active Participation

The idea here is that by being a participant in a forum, you can promote your retail business. This is actually a pretty good idea. The idea assumes that the products you sell are directly related to the forum topic, that you are an expert in the products you sell (as you should be), and that as an expert you can help other members of the forum in their efforts to buy, use, and sell the products.

For instance, suppose you sell specialized digital-camera equipment and software, which enables people to shoot high-quality panoramic photographs. You are an expert in shooting panoramic photographs, a somewhat technical aspect of photography. An online forum on panoramic photography exists. As a participant, you can help other members of this forum effectively shoot panoramic photographs.

Participation Guide

Unfortunately, participating in a forum is a hazardous affair when your objective is to promote your business. It is very easy to offend someone, and when you offend one person, it has the psychological effect of offending the entire group. Without audio and visual cues, written words have a power in conversation online that seems unnatural. You have to be very careful what you say.

Here are some guidelines to keep in mind as a participant:

1. Follow the forum rules. Don't get crosswise with the forum sponsor.

2. Never be critical, negative, sarcastic, condescending, or nasty with anyone.

3. Never say that something is right, wrong, or better. If you advocate a better way of doing something or a better product, say it is more efficient, easier, less expensive, easier to learn, etc.

4. Always be complimentary and positive with everyone.

5. Be helpful as a friendly expert.

6. Participate regularly so that everyone in the forum knows you and expects to hear form you in a timely manner on subjects within the scope of your expertise.

7. Never openly market your retail products or your business.

Make it appear that you have a great interest in and enthusiasm for the forum topic (e.g., panoramic photography) and are happy to help people with their problems large and small where appropriate.

Signature

A signature is a line(s) of text that automatically follows your body of text in a forum message. You can use a signature to show your address, publish a quote, indicate your business, or show whatever you desire. A signature can be short or huge.

Most forum sponsors have rules about signatures. Typically signatures can't be over a certain size and they can't be blatantly commercial. Follow the sponsor's rules. Keep your signature short, and don't try to make it an advertisement for your business.

Nevertheless, there's nothing wrong with stating the name of your business. You want people to know you're in a business that's related to the topic of the forum. In other words, make sure that you use a signature and make sure that the signature makes it clear to everyone that you're in a business related to the topic of the forum. For example, the following signature will work well:

Jason Smith
Panorama Photo Supplies

However, if your business name doesn't depict what you sell, you may have to elaborate:

Jason Smith
Smith Equipment & Supplies
Specializing in Panoramic Photo Supplies

Keep in mind, the longer and more commercial your signature seems, the more chance it has of offending forum members or violating sponsor guidelines.

Time Requirements

It takes time to write carefully worded messages for participation in a forum. And if you don't take the time to be careful, surely you will offend someone. Don't underestimate the time you will spend as a participant, and remember that only ongoing participation is worthwhile. Occasional participation probably won't support a reasonable marketing effort. With that in mind, only you can decide whether your participation in a forum is worth the time for your particular business and your particular products.

Every retail business is different with different opportunities. Perhaps the more specialized your products, the more it makes sense to participate in a forum(s), particularly a specialized forum(s).

If multiple forums exist on the same topic or if you have several sets of products each related to a different forum, your potential time requirements for meaningful participation will increase. Thus, you will have to set priorities. You can't do everything.

Keeping in Touch

There's another reason for participation in a forum. It helps you keep in touch with your customers. You know what they routinely talk about. This can be very enlightening and give you useful insight into your retail business.

As mentioned earlier, to do this, you don't necessarily have to be an active forum participant. You can be passive and read all the messages without ever writing one.

Non-Marketing Participation

Nothing in this chapter should be intrepreted as discouraging you from participating in a forum that enhances your professionalism. Do I think you should participate in a forum about operating an eBay business? Absolutely. But that's not marketing.

Sponsorship

When you operate a forum, you have another set of considerations to face in addition to your participation. Establishing and operating a forum is difficult, and you cannot assume that you will be successful.

Critical Mass

The first objective is to get a critical mass of participants. That appears to be easy. The typical successful forum appears to have about 50 contributors with perhaps a dozen of them more active than the others. But it's what you don't see that's important.

I had a discussion with Margaret Levine Young, author of *Poor Richard's Building Online Communities* (Top Floor Publishing, 2000) about critical mass. She estimates that most forums have about a 10:1 ratio of passive participants to active participants. That means to get 50 active participants, you have to have a forum membership of 500 people.

Without a critical mass, a forum just sputters along and doesn't do much or draw much attention. Lively discussions are few and far between, and often long periods (e.g., two days) go by without any messages at all. Without at least a dozen messages a week, a forum is dead.

Administration

Someone has to administer the forum. You can do this using software, and you can set up most forum software to be self-administering. Nonetheless, you still need to devote some attention to making sure everything runs smoothly. If you try to do this without self-administrating software, you will have a big job on your hands.

Management

Managing a forum means managing the participants. More specifically, it means policing the participants. First, you need to set up forum policies and rules. A forum is a community, and like any community, it needs guidelines to help it function well.

Second, you need to set the topic for the forum. This seems self-evident. Nevertheless, you need to establish rules that keep the discussion on topic (i.e., enforce the topic). Otherwise the forum discussion will digress into a general discussion (e.g., politics), and eventually the forum will disintegrate.

Third, you need to calm and regulate disruptive participants. People sometimes get mad at each other on forums, and it's up to you to keep things peaceful. Sometimes that means kicking unruly participants off the forum. Managing a forum properly requires sensitivity, fairness, and firmness. Experience in the diplomatic service is helpful.

Employee

Can you have an employee (or independant contractor) operate a forum for you? Sure. Obviously it can't be just anyone, however. It has to be a person with the maturity and skills to make it work. The forum will be perceived by the participants as your baby. If you don't manage it yourself, you need to find someone you can trust to do it well and do it professionally.

Archives

One of the advantages of operating a forum is that the ongoing record of participation can become content for your website. In other words, you need to archive the forum messages. The discussions of various topics will be valuable to future readers who search through the message archives looking for specific information.

Participation

And what about participating in your own forum? Nothing wrong with that. However, you will have to be extra careful. Because you are the forum sponsor (manager) and a participant too, you will find that your words are magnified considerably. Everything you say should be measured carefully to avoid offending anyone and to avoid miscommunications. See the Active Participation section above.

Cost-Effectiveness Review

My view is that forum participation is most useful when your business serves a specific specialty that coincides with the forum topic. That is, exactly what you sell fits a forum representing a niche large enough to support profitable sales but small enough to be uninviting to competition. Under such circumstances, participation can constitute a good marketing campaign. It's also a way to keep in touch with your customers.

Having said that, I am skeptical that participation in forums is generally cost-effective. Forum participation takes time. You have to write well-thought-out messages and be sensitive to other forum participants. You can't be in a hurry and do a good job. If the forum's topic is broader than the spectrum of your products, your participation may not generate significant sales.

Nor is sponsoring a forum a quick or easy path to success. It will likely take considerable time, effort, and promotion (of the forum) to get your forum participation to a critical mass. Without the critical mass, your forum is not likely to be an effective marketing tool.

All things considered, forums are probably not the place for you to spend your time and energy most effectively to generate sales. Unless you're in a narrow niche without competition, your priorities are better placed elsewhere.

19

Cross-Selling

When you give purchasing suggestions for other products to your buyers, either before a sale or after a sale, it's a cross-promotion. Generally, there two types:

Upsell Use this before a sale to suggest that the prospective buyer buy a bigger, better, and more expensive product in place of the one being purchased (e.g., eBay Store cross-promotion panel at bottom of item listing pages).

Cross-Sell Use this after a sale to suggest additional purchases of accessories, supplementary products, ancillary products, or otherwise related products (e.g., eBay Store cross-promotion panel at bottom of *Bid Confirm* and *Confirmation* pages).

With an upsell, you have to be careful that you don't give buyers the impression that you're trying to pull some sort of bait-and-switch routine. An upsell is always just a suggestion and nothing more.

A cross-sell is very effective, particularly for products that are used with multiple accessories. And even the simplist products often have accessories or related products.

Location

What constitutes a cross-selling device? Where do you place a cross-selling device? How do you enable cross-selling?

Webpage

A cross-selling device can be as simple as text in a webpage. The text makes the cross-selling offer, describes the product, and includes a link to the product's webpage and a photograph. A popular device for cross-selling is a panel that includes three or four products. You can put it a variety of places (see Figure 19.1 and read below).

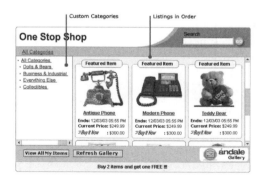

Figure 19.1 Andale Gallery, a cross-promotion panel. ©2004 Andale Inc.

Email

There are two ways to cross-sell using email. First, you can include products in the body (text) of a normal email. Again, these would be accessories or supplementary products to the product that was purchased. Included with the information would be links taking the buyer directly to the accessory products' catalog webpages in your eBay Store. You would send such an email to customers soon after a purchase. You can experiment with the time lapse between a purchase and the follow-up email. A half-day, a day, a week or some other period might work best.

Second, you can include a cross-promotion panel in an email. This would be the same panel that you use for eBay auction ads, eBay Stores, or the eBay checkout. It's a panel with three or four products together with their photographs. Normally, it would go at the bottom of the email. But, it could go anywhere in the body of the email too.

This approach to cross-selling can be used in the requisite follow-up emails for every transaction. For instance, you can include the cross-promotion panel in the original follow-up email after the ending of an auction. This is the email that you use to tell the buyer about the means of payment and the means of shipment. The cross-promotion panel email turns the email message itself into a dual-purpose email.

Newsletter

If you send out a periodic newsletter, you can customize it. For instance, you can include customer's name and other customer information inside the body (text) of the newsletter using database technology. (See Chapter 17. It includes information on mail merging.) If you can do that much, you can also include a cross-promotion panel in the newsletter based on the customer's last purchase. If your newsletter is monthly, the customer will see the cross-promotion panel no later than one month after the purchase. But, in any event, the cross-promotion panel is tailored to a customer's purchases.

This is just one of many ideas that will enable you to use a cross-promotion panel productively. With the use of the panel or with other cross-selling techniques, the sky's the limit with what you do. Cross-selling is effective when the cross-selling products are relevant and presented in a timely manner. This is a very powerful tool when used properly and efficiently.

Auction Management Services

You can easily send a follow-up email with cross-selling information in it. But with any kind of a volume of eBay retail business, that task would very quickly become burdensome and tedious. Therefore, you need an auction management service that facilitates such emails. In addition, to use the cross-promotion panel effectively, you need an auction management service that enables you to use the panel in a variety of places such as webpages, email, newsletters, and almost anywhere you can place an image.

When you choose an auction management service, keep this in mind. Carefully review what cross-selling features and devices the auction management service provides.

Expand Your Inventory

Trying to keep your eBay business simple and your inventory turning over at a high rate by having a limited number of products? That's admirable and no doubt profitable. But you might be missing some easy sales through cross-selling. Although this book is not about increasing your sales by expanding your inventory, cross-sales is an exception to the book's theme.

If you are selling products that require accessories or related products, then it makes sense to stock such items and cross-sell them. This is particularly true where the accessories and related products are substantial merchandise. For instance, if you can sell someone a $60 camera bag after selling them a $180 camera, that's good business that you don't want to pass up. OK, so you don't want to bother selling a customer 4 batteries for $3 after selling them a $180 camera. But how about selling them a pack of 40 batteries for $20?

Cost-Effectiveness Review

Cross-selling can be cost-effective if you automate it. The only way you can automate it is by using an appropriate auction management service. In others words, with the right software, it can be a cost-effective means of increasing sales.

20

Advertising

Can you use advertising to build your brand? You bet! Advertising is a traditional way to build brands, and is perhaps the most widely used and effective way to do so. That does not bode well for building your eBay brand, however, because advertising tends to be expensive. Even on the Web it tends to be expensive.

Just because it's expensive doesn't mean you shouldn't do it. It means that if you do advertise, you will want to advertise intelligently while measuring its effectiveness. This chapter covers four types of online advertising below which you can use with confidence. But that doesn't mean that other advertising schemes won't work. The Web is young and there is a lot yet to be invented. When it comes to advertising, think of the process as one long experiment. Keep track of results. Experiment more. Find out what works for your products.

Advertising Links

The Web has a unique feature, which is a compelling one for advertising: hyperlinks (links). Links appear in a different color (and with an underline). When the reader clicks on the words, the reader is magically taken to a different webpage.

Why is this important for advertising? Because link words embedded in text are rather inconspicuous. They don't interfere with reading. Yet, they can take readers off to new websites, new webpages, or even to a graphic presentation. And any one of those three can be an effective advertisement. For instance, suppose you operate a chess boutique where people can buy chess sets, chess pieces, and chess paraphernalia. You have a pleasant storefront website and would love to have people come in the front door. You also have specific webpages inside your website where people can learn about your products. Then too, you have other webpages where they can use chess tutorials. Furthermore, you have plenty of digital photographs showing your products.

Suppose some enterprising individual publishes a chess newsletter online. The possibilities follow:

1. Your storefront website could be mentioned in an article written for the newsletter. A link could bring readers directly to your storefront.

2. One of your products or one of your tutorials could be mentioned in the article. And the words that mentioned your products or tutorials could be links. That would potentially take readers right from the article to your product or tutorial webpages.

3. A reference to a photograph (of a product) that you show on your website could be made in the article, and a link could take a reader straight to a digital photograph of a product.

Provide Photographs

You might want to set up your website so that anybody who desires can "steal" your photographs. Make it easy for them to come in and take the photographs right out of your webpages.

What's in it for you? Nothing, unless there is something in your photographs indicating your brand and where your online retail store can be found. That turns your photograph from just a photograph into an advertising message.

It's easy to add text to a photograph with an image editor. Put your business name and your website URL somewhere in the photograph where it won't be distracting. It should be big enough to read but small enough to be inconspicuous.

Other websites don't actually have to steal one of your photographs to use it. They can just reference the photograph's URL in an image link in their own webpage, and your photograph will magically appear in that webpage. Make your photographs work for you by letting other people use them.

Competitors

Many eBay businesses—and other online retailers—put text across their photographs so that their competitors cannot use the photographs for selling indentical products. Unfortunately, such text is distracting, often ruins photographs, and hinders sales even if it does stymie competitors. Perhaps you can follow the sidebar above and make your photographs available to non-competitors but not to competitors. There's no foolproof way to do this. Still, if you go to the trouble to display a copyright notice, that will discourage many competitors from stealing.

The copyright notice should also contain licensing language that gives anyone—except your competitors—a right to use the images unaltered. Remember, the photographs should have your name and URL on them in an inconspicuous place.

Banner Ads

Banner ads are simply photographs or graphic artworks that are also links. Most have an advertising quality to them. When website visitors click on a banner ad, the ad takes them to another website or webpage.

Do banner ads work well? In a word, yes. At an appropriate website, banner ads can generate click-throughs. Naturally, it depends on the quality of advertising and the location as to how well a specific banner ad works, but banner ads are a proven means of generating sales leads—and ultimately sales. Although generally expensive, banner ads are often a dependable means of advertising on the Web.

Website Sections

Suppose there is a website for parlor games (FamilyGames) that's very popular. It might be effective for you to have a banner ad on such a website for your chess boutique. However, with the FamilyGames website, it's time to think big. You will want more than just a banner ad on this website. You will want a section of the FamilyGames website for yourself where you can promote your retail chess business.

There are several ways you can do this.

1. Supply a set of webpages to FamilyGames for uploading to its website.

2. Supply a set of webpages on your website but linked (both ways) to the FamilyGames website. These webpages become, in effect,

a portion of the website at FamilyGames (see Chapter 15).

3. Have FamilyGames link to your website inside an HTML frame, enabling website visitors to easily return to FamilyGames once they visit your website.

First, you can always provide webpages (or content in another format) to the FamilyGames website. FamilyGames will probably take your content (text) and copy and paste such content into templates for the FamilyGames website. In other words, FamilyGames will want to have the look and feel of the webpages at the FamilyGames website, not your website. And that's OK.

Second, you can also use a link to go from the FamilyGames website to a custom section on your website devoted to the use of FamilyGames. (Note that this link does not go to your home page.) In the custom section of your website, you can make it appear as if it is really a portion of the FamilyGames website. Since it's devoted to FamilyGames, links in the custom webpages will return website visitors back to the FamilyGames website rather than to someplace else in your website. For a better understanding of how this might work, read Chapter 15 on multi-URL websites.

Is this is a lot of trouble to go to? The more places you advertise and set up this scheme, the more trouble it will be. Does that mean it's a prohibitive marketing technique? No. It's like anything else. You can get set up digitally to maintain custom webpages quickly and efficiently using webpage templates and other digital techniques. And you have direct control of the maintenance, which you don't on the FamilyGames website. The one disadvantage to this kind of an advertising scheme is that your webpages and the custom section you devote to the FamilyGames will look different than the FamilyGames website. That may not appeal to FamilyGames.

Third, you can use a simple link on FamilyGames website that leads to your website. This is a loose association of your content on the FamilyGames website, but it's one that can be made more inclusive with the use of frames. With frames, a link can take a website visitor off the FamilyGames website and bring her to your website without leaving the FamilyGames website, in effect. Your website always appears within a frame that exists on the FamilyGames website. Although a frame can be invisible, it usually consists of a side panel with a navigation menu on it. That navigation menu is for the FamilyGames website. Thus, your website appears in the frame with the FamilyGames navigation menu, and the website visitor feels that she never left the FamilyGames website.

Is using frames a good practice? I believe there are valid reasons to use frames occasionally. But to include somebody else's website, or a portion thereof, within your own website via frames is in most cases not a good practice. It sometimes confuses people, and if it doesn't confuse them, it may irritate them when they can't seem to get out of the frame. You should probably forgo this practice unless you have a specific use for it that doesn't either confuse or irritate website visitors.

Now, in using one of the three techniques mentioned above, what can you do? Well, you may not want to provide just advertising. You may want to provide some content too.

Content

What's the prime objective of having a section on someone else's website? Why are we talking about all of these techniques and going to all of this trouble to do this? The answer is: content. You want to get a portion of your content on somebody else's website to help market your products.

The idea is that supplying content to another website is a mutually beneficial arrangement. You get some promotion value, and the other website gets free content. The other website might also collect an advertising fee from you.

Content in Action

There are two things to keep in mind here:

1. Products for sale can be content.

2. Content can be also anything discussed in Chapter 22.

The first thing you might want to ask yourself is, What's the specific benefit to the other website? The answer is simply that your content has to be relevant to the theme of the other website. If your retailing isn't relevant to the other website, then there's no point to using the techniques outlined in this section.

For instance, your chess store has great relevancy to the FamilyGames website. Chess is a popular family game. Therefore, there's content you can contribute to this website, such as a mini-catalog of chess sets. Just a little catalog not only creates content for the FamilyGames website but also provides a convenience to its website visitors.

You might also offer chess tutorials to the FamilyGames website. Many people have enough interest in chess to seek to improve their chess skills. That is, they might use your chess tutorials. Presumably using your tutorials it will eventually lead them to purchasing your products. But the tutorials also add great content to the FamilyGames website.

The content you provide makes the other website more robust and more attractive to website visitors. The content also helps you sell your products. This is a win-win arrangement, so to speak.

Indeed, this is a wonderful marketing technique. But it has one big problem. Most website owners don't have the vision to grow their website using other people's content. Therefore, in many cases you will have a sales job on your hands to convince other website operators to include your content.

Some website operators, once they agree to accommodate you, will be very sensitive to how your section of their website is set up and run—

understandably. You may have to give them a couple of different alternatives regarding how the concept can be put into effect in a way that's agreeable. Other website operators, once they understand the idea, won't care how how you set up your content, and you will be free to use the format that's most convenient for you.

Affiliates

Affiliated marketing programs fit this concept very nicely. An affiliate marketing program essentially markets and sells your products on someone else's website and pays him a commission, in effect, to use his website for your sales. Amazon.com is famous for enabling you to get paid for Amazon book sales that come in via links from your website. In that case, it's up to you to build the book catalog. However, Amazon and other online book vendors will also create a mini-catalog—what amounts to a small book store—right on your website. Of course, all of the books offered are relevant to the subject matter of your website. (See Chapter 24 for more on affiliate programs.)

As you can understand, an affiliated marketing program may be your best shot on adding content to other people's websites. In this case, the content is strictly products for sale. If you add content other than products for sale, it will be up to you to create a format acceptable to both you and the other party.

Works for You Too

Keep this concept in mind when you are building your website. It may be to your best advantage to get other people to add content to your website to make it more robust. The incentive for them will be that they can sell products and services relevant to the subject matter of your website, on your website. The benefit to you is you can build up your website to be an information center or portal—a major attractor—faster and at less expense than you would be able to without such participation. Thus, the idea of advertising (or marketing) is not only something you will find beneficial to do on other people's websites but also something that you will find beneficial to you if done on your website by someone else.

Keyword Ads

Keyword ads are for search engines. When certain keywords are used to search, ads for products relevant to the keywords appear on the pages of returns for the search. These are box ads with plain text, usually in a column on the right or left of the central column of text. For instance, Google offers its Adwords program (*https://adwords.google.com*) and eBay offers its Keywords program (*http://www.ebaykeyworks.com* – see more details below).

This is Web advertising that works. It's advertising that's appropriate for experimentation because it's not necessarily a large investment. You can buy as much or as little as you want.

Think about what this book has instructed. First, Google is a major gateway to ecommerce perhaps as big or bigger than eBay. Second, Froogle will be as big or bigger than Google before long as a gateway to ecommerce. Third, eBay itself has become a major gateway to ecommerce, not just another marketplace on the Web. And what do they all have in common? They all offer keyword advertising, and keyword advertising has proven to be effective. Can't ask for much more than that.

If you are going to advertise, keyword advertising should be your first stop, that is, your first consideration. You may decide to do other types of advertising instead, but you should at least investigate and consider keyword advertising.

Overture (*http://overture.com*), now owned by Yahoo, and FindWhat (*http://findwhat.com*) are examples of the many additional keyword ad programs that may be worthwhile.

Compensation

You can pay for links, banner ads, or advertising sections with a monthly fee, a click-through fee (based on how many people click to see the linked webpages), or even on an exchange basis.

Along with compensation comes accountability. When you advertise, you want to make sure that the other website that you are paying is accountable for advertising performance. There are plenty of link and banner ad programs. They are programs that will keep track of the click-throughs on advertising and give a periodic report (e.g., once a week). Don't pay for advertising without such accountability being offered as part of the advertising package.

For keyword advertising on eBay, Google, Froogle, or other major ecommerce gateways, you pay for click-throughs. This is know as "pay per click" or PPC advertising. You can buy as many or as few click-throughs as you want. Each portal has its own payment scheme. But advertising is not limited to only affluent businesses. Any business can buy some advertising, that is, some number of click-throughs. Moreover, you can buy advertising in small enough quantities to experiment before you commit yourself to larger expenditures. Keyword advertising (PPC advertising) works well, and the payment schemes for keyword advertising make its use flexible.

Affiliate marketing is different. Keep in mind that when you control the operation of the sales effort, as you do with affiliate marketing programs, it is you who provides the accountability to let the other website know how many click-throughs or sales have been made—and pay accordingly. If you can't do that, you're unlikely to find participating websites.

eBay Advertising

eBay offers several advertising programs that may help you increase your sales cost-effectively.

Co-Op Advertising

eBay has a co-op advertising program. Go to *http://www.ebaycoopadvertising.com* for details. You can get reimbursed for a portion of the advertising expenses for advertising your eBay merchandise. There are restrictions, but if you spend a significant amount on advertising, this presents an opportunity to recoup some of your costs.

eBay Keyword Ads

Wouldn't it be great to be able to advertsie on eBay itself? This is one way you can do it. Advertising right on eBay with text-box ads. Your ads for your products appear at the top of listing pages for lists of items under the keywords you choose. You pay for click-throughs. Go to *https://ebay.admarketplace.net/ebay/servlet/ebay* for full information on eBay keyword advertising on eBay.

One great feature of this program is that you can set your own budget. You won't get charged more than you want to spend. Of course, once you reach your budget amount, your ads no longer appear.

Keywords for Titles

You can use the eBay keyword ads process to discover fruitful keywords to use in your eBay auction ad titles.

As mentioned earlier, keyword advertising can be very effective. However, you need to determine whether eBay keyword advertising is as effective as Google or Froogle keyword advertising (Adwords). Only your experiments will tell.

Offline Advertising

Advertising offline works fine for ecommerce on the Web, if you can find an advertising medium that fits your products. It costs money and is usually expensive, but that doesn't mean it can't be cost-effective.

Don't rule it out without evaluating specific opportunities that seem to have promise.

What many ecommerce businesses have found when advertising offline is that many orders come in by telephone. Yes, there are still people who aren't connected to the Internet or who don't find shopping online convenient. If you advertise offline, you'd better have some order-takers ready by your phones.

Cost-Effectiveness Review

Arranging links and banner ads for no fee, which is possible, might be cost-effective. It's possible, however, you will spend too much time trying to find free websites, and cost-effectiveness will go down the drain.

If you are willing to pay for links, banner ads, and PPC advertising, the cost-effectiveness will depend on the results. To measure the cost-effectiveness, you will need to know the results. Consequently, you will want to make sure that any advertising you do is accompanied by periodic reports on performance.

Cost-effectiveness is more difficult to evaluate for using a section of another website. It will take more work to prepare the webpages than a banner ad, and you are unlikely to get any reports on overall performance. However, if the other website has high traffic and is closely relevant, it might prove to be a great marketing opportunity.

If you create an affiliation with another website, you can count your results yourself (i.e., sales made via the affiliate website), but it is you who will need to provide the periodic result reports to the affiliate website. The cost-effectiveness will depend on the degree of automation provided by your affiliate software (see Chapter 24).

21

Publishing

Writing is a great way to create content. Linking audio or video presentations may also work well for you. Once your writing is done or your presentations made, publishing them can become a powerful means of marketing. I'm not talking about advertising or promotional materials. I'm talking about creating information that's useful to your customers when they use your products.

If you feel you can't write well enough to take advantage of the ideas in this chapter, you might consider two possible alternatives. First, you can try your hand at writing, and then hand off what you've done to a competent editor. With some heavy editing, you may be able to write better than you thought you could.

Always Edit

Even if you write well, you need to have someone edit your writing so that you produce a commercially viable writing product.

Second, you can hire someone to write content for you. You don't have to look far to find good writers. You may be able to find an English major at your local college. You can contact a local writing club to find people that write in a professional manner. And it's not difficult to find good writers for hire on the Internet. In order to get the most for your money, you need to provide a hired writer with a product similar to that which you expect to create. This is, provide an existing example that the writer can imitate. Additionally, provide an outline of the subject matter. The more detailed the outline, the faster the writing will go and the less expensive the writing will be.

If you want to create writing products, but you're not sure exactly what you want, a good writer may be able to help you conceptualize the final product. That means the writer will spend more time with you and thus expect to get paid more.

If you are a good writer and you're too busy tending to business to take the time to write, hiring a writer may be a good choice for you.

If your products require technical writing, you will need to find a technical writer. If, on the other hand, your products require little technical expertise to use or operate, almost any writer can probably do the job for you. Professional writers usually have a wide range of interests and a wide range of quasi-expertise. They can easily use their skills for writing about products that are new to them.

In the chapter sections that follow, I will outline some of the writing devices that you can use to promote your eBay business. In addition, I will cover audio, video and multimedia presentations.

What's the Point?

Before I get started here, remind yourself that content attracts new buyers and keeps customers hanging around. Attractive content in the context of selling products usually means informational presentations that instruct how to buy, use, maintain, and sell the products. And where does this content go? Most likely it will be located on an independent website that you integrate into your eBay Store and About Me as outlined in Chapter 15. Read Chapter 22 for more details on the use of content to attract potential buyers. And now back to publishing the content.

Written Presentations

To save space in the book and because an eBay business is an online business, the following sections on written presentations will be about digital presentations, not about printed products.

However, if you have a need to print products, you can take a digital product to a printer and have it printed. This is usually easy to do with an appropriate digital product. For instance, if a PDF file is well type-set, a printer can print it as is, and it will look pretty good. Many different types of digital documents can be converted to PDFs.

But for the most part, printing is expensive whereas publishing digitally is not, once you've created the content. So, this chapter will focus on publishing digitally.

Normal Documents

Normal documents include reports, white papers, newsletters, user manuals, tutorials, product specifications, surveys, data sheets, articles, quick-start instructions, directories, checklists, and resources. Perhaps the best way to create these is with a word processor such as Microsoft Word. You will want to make sure to nicely typeset them in Word according to traditional typesetting standards so that the documents are attractive, easy to read, and of commercial quality.

The two best ways to publish digitally are with webpages or Acrobat pages (also known as PDFs). Word will automatically take your word-processor document and convert it into a webpage. Even if you don't use that webpage, you can take the body of text inside that webpage and cut and paste it into a webpage template that someone has designed for you. Consequently, once you complete your writing in Word (and have it edited), it doesn't take much to turn it into an attractive webpage.

To create Acrobat pages (PDFs), you must use Adobe's Acrobat Distiller, an expensive program. It will take a word-processor document and replicate the way it looks very accurately into a PDF. Each PDF is a self-contained document. That means it will show whatever it replicates. For instance, although a webpage requires the font you used in the original document to show that document the way you typeset it, a PDF replicates the fonts so that the fonts used do not need to be present in a website visitor's computer.

Using Typefaces on the Web

The typeface fonts that you use in a webpage (HTML document) must reside on the user's computer. Because you can't count on all users having the same fonts that you have on your computer, you have to stick with standard (default) fonts when you're making webpages. The standard serif fonts are Times New Roman for the PC and Times for the Mac. Standard sanserif fonts are Arial for the PC and Helvetica for the Mac. Using these fonts for your webpages ensures that everybody sees your webpages the way you've typeset them.

Once you have created content, either a webpage or a PDF, you can use it on websites simply by linking to it. In the case of the webpage, you simply link to a webpage where people can read your content. To link to a PDF, you simply name the PDF file as the URL in your link, and the Web will take the user directly to the PDF. Because PDFs require Acrobat Reader for your website visitors to see them, your website visitors will have to have Acrobat installed on their computers.

There are sure to be readers who don't have Acrobat installed, however, and you will need to provide a link for them to go to Adobe's website to download the free software. This is not something to worry about, as most people already have Acrobat Reader installed.

Email

You can also put your writings in an email document. Most email programs handle plain-text documents. You can copy and paste text out of Word right into an email message. The text will appear in the plain-text format (otherwise known as ASCII format).

Copy and Paste

When you copy and paste into an email message, you need to review the text in the email message. You may need to make some adjustments to the formatting to make the text look right.

Many email programs today accommodate HTML text too. That is, you can copy and paste from an HTML document into an email message to create an email message that looks like a webpage. As you probably know from the many HTML messages that you've received, this doesn't always work the way it's supposed to. It's something you have to do very carefully, or else find somebody knowledgeable to do it for you. The benefits to your readers of doing it this way is that it creates not only a more attractive email message but one that can include graphics, digital photographs, and so forth.

What's a primary benefit of email? With email you can send your writings where you want them to go. With PDFs and webpages, your customers have to come to your website to see them. Having said that, however, I should mention that you can also attach a webpage or a PDF to an email message and send it to your customers.

eBooks

eBooks are easy to make. First you convert your writing to HTML. Then you convert it from HTML form into an ebook. This is easy to do using a freeware conversion program such as OverDrives's Reader Works Standard. Then someone can see and read the ebook in the Microsoft ebook reader.

For PDF ebooks, there used to be separate Adobe Acrobat ebook reader. Those readers have been merged into one reader in version 6.0 and above. Consequently, any PDF document that you make with Acrobat Distiller is, in effect, an ebook. It may not look like an ebook, but Adobe Reader gives it all the attributes of an ebook automatically. To make any PDF document look like an ebook, all you have to do is give it a nicely designed color front page, a title page, and all the other attributes of a book. Then with Acrobat Reader, people will be able to use it like an ebook.

Do you have to go to all the trouble of putting your ebooks into two different formats, Microsoft and Adobe? That's a tough question to answer. If the document really is an ebook, and you intend it to be an ebook, it might be best for you to publish it using both formats. Nonetheless, Acrobat is the most popular form for ebooks, and you can probably cover the territory just by publishing your ebook in the PDF format.

Audio and Video Presentations

Although one writer can create a lot of content with just writing, audio and video presentations usually take teams of people to produce or at least an individual who has mastered many different digital skills. Consequently, audio and video presentations are usually more expensive to produce and publish than written presentations. I am not going to cover them in great detail in this book as they are media probably beyond the budgets of most small businesses.

Audio

You create audio by recording voice or music either in a quiet place or in a studio. Recording high-quality voice does not require expensive equipment nor an elaborate environment. Still, you have to know what you're doing to turn out a good product. If you want to create low-cost audio content (voice), find a small radio station and use its resources for your production.

Music requires expensive equipment and audio engineers who know what they're doing. Creating music is not a project to be taken lightly or on a light pocketbook. Fortunately, there's no need to create music. There is plenty of great stock music available. You can buy the music for use in your content and in the digital format you need.

What do you do when you have a presentation finished? You can either put it on a CD or a DVD and distribute it to potential customers. However, the least expensive way to publish it is to put it on the Web. For use on the Web, the audio file needs to be compressed into a format that's usable by either the Microsoft Media Player, Real Player, or QuickTime Player. The compressed file is not downloaded all at once. Rather, it streams into a website visitor's computer and plays as it streams. A website visitor must have Real Player or QuickTime Player installed, which can be downloaded from the Real or Apple website for free. Microsoft Media Player, which comes with Microsoft's operating systems, will play the streaming audio also. A website visitor starts the streaming usually by clicking on a link in a webpage.

Video

Video requires at least a cameraman and a professional digital video camera. High-quality productions often require more equipment and personnel. The editing requires heavy-duty PC hardware and software. All in all, it tends to be an expensive proposition. Even if you can find one person who has all the production skills and equipment—not that difficult—such a person normally commands a high price. And remember too, when you produce video, you also have to produce audio. It's a double medium, unless you want to imitate silent films.

Audio-Video-Written Content

Did you note that I've discussed the technical aspects of producing audio and video? Production costs are costs in addition to the cost of actually creating the content. You need someone—perhaps yourself—to create the content. Then you need others to produce it. This is different (and more expensive) than writing where the technical aspects of production are normally not a significant consideration.

For example, let's assume you are the creator. You are a chess expert. You operate a retail chess store on eBay. And you want to create a beginner's chess tutorial that customers and prospective buyers can use on the Web. You believe the tutorial will attract people to your chess storefront where they will buy something.

First, you can write a tutorial and publish it as a webpage. If you can't write well, you can hire someone inexpensively. Then you can put the writing into a webpage template, and voila! You have a tutorial. Beginners can read it online and get some tips on how to play chess.

Second, you can make an audio tutorial by making an audio recording. You can outline the content for the recording and give the audio performance yourself. Unless you have a thousand dollars' worth of recording hardware and software and have mastered the basics of audio engineering, however, you will need someone else to make the recording, edit it, and compress it for Web use. If you don't perform yourself, you will need to hire a professional voice instead to give the performance. In addition, you will need to write a script for the performance or, more likely, hire a script writer to do it for you. The costs for an audio tutorial can mount up quickly.

Third, you can make a video tutorial by making a video recording. This is similar to making an audio presentation except that you have two media to handle (audio and video) in addition to creating the content and giving the performance. The costs for a video tutorial will likely exceed that of an audio tutorial by a generous margin.

Accordingly, you can understand that writing is an efficient and inexpensive medium, while audio or video usually cost significantly more.

Multimedia Presentations

Multimedia presentations use more than one medium. An important thing to remember is that the Web itself is multimedia. You can include almost anything in a webpage.

Text

That you can use text in a webpage is self-evident. Remember, however, that HTML enables you to use hyperlinks to include all the information anywhere on the Web in your webpages. This is impossible in printed text and opens wonderful new content-making opportunities for you, just using text.

Web Audio

To use audio on the Web, a website visitor clicks on a link to download it. The digital audio must be compressed to stream. That is, it plays (streams) *as* a website visitor downloads it, *not after* she downloads it. Web audio is underused on the Web. If you can create and perform an audio presentation and get it produced inexpensively, it can be a wonderful and worthwhile addition to your website content.

Web Video

Video is like audio. It must stream to be used. Website visitors click on a link and then watch the video on a small screen in the webpage.

Frame-Rate

Full frame-rate for video is 30 frames per second. The frame-rate for streaming video on the Web is about half that. Someday when everyone has a more powerful computer and a broadband connection, streaming video will run at full frame-rate in a larger window. Then it will be more attractive and more compelling to use.

Web video is perhaps too ambitious for small businesses to use for promotion. On the other hand, some types of information must appear on video because it is awkward to convey the information in any other way (e.g., golf lessons).

Embedded Programming

No helpful device is more overlooked on the Web than embedded programming. Through the use of CGI scripts, Java applets, and other programming systems, you can create almost any functionality you desire in a webpage at your website. (If you're not a programmer, you can hire one.) You can provide an embedded program that does anything from simple calculations to word processing. These are all used inside a Web browser.

According to Larry Chase (*http://larrychase.com*), a leading Web-marketing consultant, simple calculators are the best attractors on the Web. That's good news for you. The easiest (and least expensive) device for a programmer to program is a mathematical formula. For instance, a mortgage payment calculator is very easy to program. An attractive interface takes longer to program than the calculator itself.

Is there something your customers and potential buyers need to calculate? If so, you can provide a custom calculator inexpensively for them and thereby provide an extraordinary convenience for them.

Auction Management Service

An auction management service provides plenty of programming power through a Web browser and is a good example of embedded programming. A variety of embedded programs make up the total service.

So, what kind of a calculator might you create for your chess storefront customers? How about a timer, one that measures the time limit for each player to make a move? That would be easy enough to program, although it would be a bit awkward to have to be near your PC while playing chess. On the other hand, its use might inspire players to buy a more convenient physical timer from you.

Technically speaking, I suppose embedded programming is not a medium. Nonetheless, it is an important cornerstone of the multimedia system that makes up the Web. Calculators and other programs (applications) can be helpful to people and will draw attention to your website.

What to Avoid

Don't attempt to duplicate a certain medium for publication on the Web. For instance, don't create a half-hour streaming audio presentation to duplicate the concept of an audio tape and then have it play in a webpage. Rather break up your presentation into stand-alone audio modules which together make up the entire presentation. If possible mix up the media in a webpage (e.g., audio modules and text modules). Keep things interesting for website visitors. Enable them to digest your presentation in small bites.

And Now for the Finale

What have I completely left out thus far that can brighten up your text presentation? Digital photographs! Photographs and other digital graphics can make webpages and PDFs seem like full-color magazines. Inexpensively! If you do a text presentation, sprinkle in some digital color photographs here and there to create impressive and professional content.

For instance, with a little practice and perhaps the aid of a book on photography, you could create informative color digital photographs of a chess board and chess pieces for a chess tutorial. And you could do it yourself inexpensively.

Cost-Effectiveness Review

Content created with text or embedded programming can be cost-effective for creating attractions (attractors) to your website as part of your marketing program. And don't forget the digital photographs. Audio and video is best left to larger businesses that can afford the extra cost. Publishing content can be a powerful attractor.

22

Web Portals

What's a Web portal? I'm going to give you my definition. It's a website that acts as a gateway to a type of product, an activity, a profession, a business process, an industry, or any one of a number of other things of interest to people. Let's call the thing of interest the topic of the portal. For instance, if you created a Web portal for mountain climbers, the topic of the portal would be mountain climbing.

What can you expect at a Web portal? Everything! That is, everything that's relevant to the topic of the portal. Why is a portal important for online marketing? Because it's an attractor. It brings people in.

189

Let's take a look at what we might expect to find at a Web portal for mountaining climbing:

1. Tutorials on various climbing techniques

2. Newsletter with articles and photographs on climbing

3. Instructions and maps for climbing routes on various mountains

4. Checklists of equipment needed for various types of climbs

5. Reviews of new products

6. Climbing trip reports

7. Travel facilities available near climbing sites

8. Information on wilderness first aid

9. Workout techniques for getting in shape to climb

10. eBooks on climbing topics

11. Directories of people interested in climbing arranged by locale

12. List of mountain-climbing clubs in the US

13. List of mountain-climbing schools

14. Audio interviews with leading mountain climbers

15. Tutorial on reading clouds to predict weather

16. Lists of links to other websites relevant to mountain climbing

All this and much more. But what did we leave out? Lists of links to online retail vendors of mountaineering clothing and equipment. In fact, if you were a mountaineering retailer on eBay and operated this portal, you would use the portal as an attractor for your online retail sales (e.g., eBay, eBay Store, Froogle, etc.). There wouldn't be a list of retail vendors of mountaineering stuff. You would be the only vendor on the list.

Everything

The ideal portal includes everything relevant to the topic of the portal. Why is this a good idea for online retailing? Or, more specifically, why is this a good idea for you?

It may not be. You have to evaluate the retail situation in regard to the topic. For instance, suppose you are a mountaineering retailer. You may not want to do a mountain-climbing portal for some or all of the following reasons:

- There are already too many mountain-climbing portals.

- You're not an expert mountain climber and don't feel confident that you can create or collect the amount of content it takes to operate a robust portal.

- You are so busy with your online mountaineering retail sales that you don't have time to create and operate a portal.

- You sell only mountaineering clothing (not equipment), and mountain climbing is too broad a topic for you to support with a portal.

If the above are true, what's the answer for you? Well, one answer is to create a portal that's more narrow in its scope; that is, the topic is more narrow and more manageable.

Suppose you create and operate a mountaineering clothing portal. You have more closely tailored your portal to your retail business. You have narrowed the scope of the content you need to create or collect for the portal. You have less competition from other portals. And if you're not an expert, you can learn about mountaineering clothing faster than you can learn about the full scope of mountain climbing.

The goal is to assemble enough content in one website so as to be an attractor to potential customers. If you have a niche into which you are selling, a Web portal may support your sales quite well.

Gradually

But lets look at one more issue: You're too busy with sales to take the time to build a portal. Yet good retailers always look ahead and do things today to maintain or increase sales in the future. A Web portal is a way to do that. You may need to take time now to ensure the future success of your eBay retail business.

Can you develop a strategy to build a portal slowly? That makes sense. For instance, suppose you add only content to your portal that will be as fresh in five years as it is today. (An explaination of why a double-faced Dacron polyester fleece is a safe frabric for outdoor use written in 1985 would be as accurate and timely today as when it was written.) You try to add something every month. You can gradually build up your portal, but the content will have a timeless quality to it. After three or four years, your portal will look pretty impressive and presumably will be a sales-producing attraction.

The Partial Portal

A portal is an ambitious project. It's most likely to be done by a person who's an expert and goes into the retail business. After all, an expert can create content or may already have some usable content. An expert certainly knows how and where to collect appropriate content.

But if you're not an expert or don't have the time, what's another alternative? Certainly the idea of a portal works to some extent even if you don't go whole hog with it. In other words, add content to your website that will attract the sort of people who are your potential buyers. Good content will attract people even if it isn't a comprehensive portal. Indeed, assuming your content (topic) is in line with your retail sales, providing your customers and potential buyers with information related to your products is great customer service.

Content

Certainly Web portals draw on the information provided in some of the other chapters in this book, particularly Chapter 21 on publishing. Relevant content is an attractor. Whether you present it in a Web portal, a partial portal, or just as an occasional feature of your website, content attracts.

Attractor or What?

The assumption of this chapter is that you will use content on the topic of the portal as an attractor to generate more sales. The Web portal is the ultimate expression of content as an attractor. But that's not the only use. Content that generates sales also provides customer service both before and after a sale. So, there is a huge dimemsion of customer service in any Web portal.

Implementation

How do you implement the portal idea or how do you add content to your retail sales effort and still remain an eBay retailer? Read Chapter 15 on developing a multi-URL website.

Affiliation

Rather than creating a Web portal, it may be a better idea to join and support one that already exists. Be an active affiliate. Support the portal with money (advertising dollars) and also contribute content. Have your own section on the portal website, if possible. In order to get recognition for your participation, you need to do something more than just advertise. If you appear to be one of the "owners" of the portal due to your presence on the portal, you will get more sales than just through banner ads.

Web Mall

A Web mall is not the same as a Web portal. A Web mall is normally a shopping center on the Web (covered in Chapter 24) and does not necessarily present content related to any of the mall storefronts.

If you find a relevant Web portal in which to participate, don't be put off by the fact that some of your competitors are also affiliated. A collection of identical retailers in one place becomes an attractor in and of itself. And besides, the competition will keep you on your toes.

Cost-Effectiveness Review

I believe that the Web portal idea can provide a lot of bang for the buck. But it really depends on your situation and the niche in which you sell. The portal idea is a customer-service idea as well as an attractor idea, and it's hard to go wrong with customer service.

If you're selling in a broad market or niche, a Web portal may be too ambitious for you. If you're an expert selling in a narrow niche, a Web portal may be just your cup of tea.

You have some flexibility in what you can do. You can take the gradual approach, do a partial portal, or make an affiliation. The point is to help your customers by including content related to your products that they can use . The important thing to remember about a portal is that it's a long-term marketing technique that works day after day. An investment in some long-term content will pay off in the long-term, but you probably won't see results next week.

23

International Selling

Want to increase your sales 30 percent in a hurry? Try global sales. How do you sell internationally? You simply accept bids from buyers abroad on eBay US. Surprisingly a lot of sellers don't do this. That's why I've included a chapter in this book on global selling. However, this chapter doesn't cover the full scope of international selling.

eBay Global the Smart Way is a separate book, written with co-author Ron Ubels, a customs broker, that covers the following topics:

- Selling to consumers abroad on eBay US and on eBays abroad

- Buying on eBays abroad to find products to import and sell on eBay US

- Importing products in bulk to sell on eBay US

- Exporting in bulk for further distribution via sales on eBay US to consumers abroad and via sales on eBays abroad

In this chapter, I will cover simply selling to buyers from abroad who bid on the items you are selling on eBay US. This will be the simplified version of what you get in *eBay Global the Smart Way*, but it will get you off to a good start building your confidence in making global sales.

Extracurricular Problems

There are two major problems you have over and above the normal procedures you use for selling to buyers within the US. The first is payment. How do you make sure you get paid? The second is customs. How to make sure your item will get through customs in the country in which the buyer lives.

A third potential problem is shipment. However, shipment is not really a problem. It's easy to ship internationally. Shipment is only a problem from the point of view that it costs more to ship internationally than it does to ship within the US. So, I won't dwell on shipping as a problem. Nonetheless, you will have to figure the higher costs of shipping into your business calculations when you develop a marketing plan for items that includes selling them to people abroad.

Receiving Payment

Receiving payment from abroad isn't really so much different than receiving payment from buyers in the US. The real difference is in customer service. For instance, if you wait for a customer's check to clear in the US, it happens in a reasonably short period of time. Once it clears, you can ship the product for which you have been paid.

Checks from abroad, however, do not clear so quickly. Consequently, you may have to wait several weeks for the check to clear before you can ship the item with the confidence that you've been paid for it. This is not great customer service, but you have to follow this procedure to make sure that you get paid.

Of course, checks are not the only means of payment either for US buyers or for buyers abroad. A popular means of international payment is the postal money order—known as the international money order. If you become familiar with international money orders, you can accept them as a means of payment. Western Union money orders are also a workable means of payment. Unfortunately, Western Union money orders are expensive. It may not be productive to insist that your buyers abroad use them. Regardless of what they cost, however, there are lots of people who seem to use Western Union money orders.

PayPal is probably the best alternative of the payment methods for receiving payment from abroad. PayPal now operates in 37 countries and is expanding. PayPal can be considered a safe means of payment, and if you're selling to buyers in one of the countries where PayPal is established, you should have little trouble getting your customers to pay via PayPal. Unfortunately, there are another 140 countries where potential buyers may buy your products and where PayPal is not yet available.

Credit cards, which are a relatively safe means of payment in the US, are a risky means of receiving payment from buyers in many countries abroad. Receiving payment via credit cards from the industrial nations of Europe and elsewhere where banking rules, regulations, and traditions are well established should not be a problem. For other countries, be extra cautious. For more information on treating credit card payment cautiously, read *eBay Business the Smart Way* Second Edition.

Always maintain a higher standard for payment acceptance procedures for items you are selling which go for a high price (i.e., big ticket items). You can probably weather being burned on several small items as you build your experience in global selling. But you don't want to be burned on a big ticket item. For big ticket items you might even want to make your sale contingent on verifications. And then give yourself several days to get the verifications you need for a confident receipt of payment.

Whatever standards and guidelines you set up in regard to receiving payment from buyers abroad, you need to state those in your eBay auction ad. Otherwise buyers from abroad will assume that whatever your normal policies are for receipt of payment are also the policies that will apply to them. So, if you do have separate policies that apply to buyers from abroad—and you should—state them in your eBay auction ad. But don't freeze out buyers from abroad. You will be cutting your potential sales by a significant percentage.

Customs Procedures

Your primary job in exporting items that you sell to buyers abroad is simply providing the proper documentation for them to import the items. Unfortunately with 180 or so different countries with different requirements for paperwork, this is not necessarily a straightforward job. Fortunately, there is a way to deal with this. It's not foolproof. Nonetheless, it's practical. You simply enclose some generic documents with the item, when you ship it, in the hope that it will clear customs in the buyer's country. For most countries it will work, but for other countries additional documentation may be required.

If additional documentation is required, customs will likely notify the buyer who will then notify you. At that point, you can supply the additional documentation. However, as you can imagine, that will cause a delay in the delivery of the item. Such a delay is not good customer service.

To be more precise, you can read *eBay Global the Smart Way* for access to the information you need to export items correctly to every country. As a practical matter, however, you can get by just by enclosing the standard documents, which are outlined in the following subsection.

Required Documents

You can get by with two documents in most countries. They are:

Commercial Invoice This contains a description of the item and the value (sale price). It is provided in place of the customs invoice required by most countries.

Certificate of Origin This document states where the item was manufactured.

NAFTA Statement If you export or import between the NAFTA countries (US, Canada, Mexico), you use the NAFTA statement instead of the certificate of origin.

There are standard form for all of these documents. You can also generate them with a computer program, which works efficiently when you export routinely each day or each week.

Attaching the Documents

You put the customs documents in an envelope and attach the envelope to the outside of the package for the item you are sending. Label the envelope "Customs Documents". Use an address label separate and in a different place on the package from the attached envelope. Now you're all set to send the item via any shipping method that you choose.

Shipping

Shipping via courier is fast and safe. But it's expensive. Shipping via the post office can be the most inexpensive, but it's not necessarily speedy. Consequently, you have to develop a strategy for shipping when you sell to customers abroad. For big ticket items, shipping by courier may not be a problem. The costs of shipping internationally as a percentage of total costs may still be low. For inexpensive items, however, you may have serious customer service problems on your hands when it comes to expensive shipping. The post office may be the only reasonable way to ship and keep the shipping costs low enough to make sense as a percentage of overall costs.

Check out the courier websites at the URLs below to determine typical shipping costs abroad.

DHL, *http://www.dhl-usa.com/IntlSvcs/IntlSvcsHome .asp?nav=InternationalService*

FedEx, *http://fedex.com/us*

Purolator, *http://www.purolator.com/crossborder/index.html*

UPS, *http://www.ups.com/content/us/en/resources/advi sor/index.html*

Checking out the shipping costs of the couriers will give you a better overall perspective on what your shipping strategy should be.

Go to the post office website to determine the international postage rates for various countries to which you anticipate you may ship products. That will give you a better overall perspective on how postal service shipping may accommodate your less expensive items. Keep in mind that once the item passes from the US Postal Service to a postal service in a foreign country, it becomes unknown how well the postal system will perform. In the first-world countries, you can expect the postal service to be efficient. In many of the third-world countries, the postal service is a question mark. Thus, how fast your item will be delivered, particularly in third-world countries, is a question that's difficult to answer.

The post offices for the US and Canada are:

USPS, *http://usps.com*

Canada Post, *http://www.canadapost.ca/segment-e.asp*

One problem in shipping via the US Postal Service is that no insurance is provided. Although the couriers provide minimal insurance and offer the election of buying additional insurance fairly inexpensively, the Postal Service does not provide insurance. Getting insurance from the Postal Service tends to be somewhat expensive. However, there are other vendors that will provide shipping insurance significantly cheaper than the Postal Service. You will probably want to check into these insurance vendors to determine how you can provide protection for your customers at a reasonable cost.

Cost-Effectiveness Review

Is selling to customers abroad cost-effective? You bet! The real effort is in getting set up. Once you are set up to ship to customers abroad, actually doing it is just a matter of routine. It's a little extra busy work but does not require a lot of additional effort. In fact, the more you can automate the busy work using digital techniques—such as standardized digital customs documents—the easier the fulfillment routine will be. This is clearly a means of expanding your market and expanding your sales that you will be foolish to overlook.

Again, a reminder regarding specific products. Some large and heavy products may not be suitable for overseas sales simply because they cost too much to ship via courier. For instance, an 80-pound computer monitor that you sell for $200 may cost more than that to ship overseas. So, when it comes to cost-effectiveness, you have to develop a strategy for selling abroad by analyzing the shipping costs and relating such costs to your products and the prices of your products.

24

Other Online-Marketing Techniques

The other online-marketing techniques covered in this catchall chapter range from automated techniques that cost little or nothing to more traditional techniques that cost you time or money. A few of them are merely familiar variants of advertising. They will all work to one degree or another. It's up to you to determine which of them will work for your products. Let me restate that. It's up to you to *experiment* to determine which will work for your products.

At the end of the chapter is a brief summary of what you can do to evaluate any online marketing technique to get a better idea of its cost-effectiveness.

Web Malls

Web malls have generally been unsuccessful on the Web. Although they seem like a great idea—after all, they work well in local geographical areas—they have not been able to attract much attention on the Web. Therefore, I don't see them as a significant force in ecommerce.

If you look at AOL in store (*http://www.in-store.com*) and MSN Shopping (*http://shopping.msn.com*), you will see that they are significant shopping malls. You can argue that these malls are successful. I will argue however, that considering the amount of time, energy, and effort behind those malls, they have been remarkably unsuccessful compared to eBay. Indeed, considering the huge amount of capital behind them, it is surprising that these malls have not become a dominant factor in ecommerce.

One of the problems is that online malls typically charge retailers such a high amount to participate that the retailers have to charge high prices in order to operate viable businesses. The consequence of such a policy is that online retailers must charge as much for products as they would in a bricks and mortar store. They have no advantage in competing with physical stores other than perhaps convenience for people that don't like to go shopping. In effect, they rob ecommerce of its very essence: the capability to reduce overhead and charge lower prices. Without this capability (advantage), ecommerce is not very competitive and is less viable. That's one of the primary reasons why eBay—with its economical fees and generally lower prices for products—has run away with all of the business.

What are malls good for? I would argue nothing. If you place a store in AOL in store or MSN Shopping, you will be sure to sell some merchandise. The real question, however, is whether such an operation will be profitable and scalable. In too many cases, it won't.

There are hundreds of other malls around the Internet in which you can establish a storefront. Maybe thousands. Name one. I can't name one. That leads me to believe that such malls are not worth your consideration.

Is there any reason for joining a Web mall? If a Web mall is inexpensive and provides you with everything you need for a storefront, it might be worth your consideration. The things you would look for would be storefront webpages, a catalog, a shopping cart, and a checkout process. These are essential things you need to run your own independent website, and if you can do it through a shopping mall at an inexpensive price, that might be the way to go. Keep in mind, however, that most of the auction management services—which you should be using—provide many of the digital devices that you need for ecommerce. Most capable auction management services provide templates for webpages, a catalog, a shopping cart, and a checkout mechanism. In fact, many of them provide their own Web mall too.

PayPal As an Auction Management Service

PayPal is not limited to eBay. In fact, eBay bought it in 2002 after it had already become very successful. Today it continues to serve ecommerce well beyond eBay. For that reason, PayPal has developed its own ecommerce management capabilities and even competes with eBay. One of the features of PayPal management services is the PayPal mall.

Could it come to pass that the PayPal mall will someday become a successful mall? Because of its situation, that's entirely possible.

Specialized Malls

If you can find a specialized mall that specializes only in the kind of products and services that you sell, it may be a strategic place to locate your website retail business. By virtue of having many similar retailers in the same place, such a mall is likely to be a legitimate attraction (attractor). After all, retail sales are an attractor, and if you can get many different retail operations satisfying the same needs, you can create a major attractor.

Comsumers love choice. Thus, if you could put all of the scuba-diving shops on the Web in one mall, it would, in effect, become a huge attractor for those who enjoy scuba diving. The primary problem with doing this is that most scuba-diving shops do not want to be in the same mall with all of their competitors. As a result, they tend to follow the geographical model of one scuba-diving shop in each mall across the country. But that doesn't work well on the Web.

The Portal as a Specialized Mall

As I outlined in Chapter 22 on portals, my definition of a portal is an information center. If you put all of the information about scuba diving into a portal and added a half dozen scuba-diving stores, the scuba-diving stores would be a great additional attractor for the portal. And they would likely enjoy good sales. In fact a portal, according to my definition, should include good shopping, and therefore it's valid to look at any specialized portal as a potential specialized mall.

On the other hand, if you were to create a specialized mall that included many Web scuba-diving shops, you would certainly want to take the time and effort to add something to such a mall. What you would add is content. That is, tutorials and other information on scuba diving would benefit customers. Thus, a specialized mall would start to look like my definition of a portal.

Let me point out, however, that in this section I've used the word *specialized* malls. These ideas are not relevant to general malls. And, in fact, these ideas do not work for general malls. Also note that you cannot find very many specialized malls on the Web.

Cost-Effectiveness Review

Web malls are not cost-effective for marketing. Some may be cost-effective as an inexpensive place to establish an ecommerce storefront location on the Web, but most will not bring in business for you. The ones that will bring in business are expensive.

eBay as a Mall

You could say that eBay is a huge mall with over 22 million items for sale. The auction portion of eBay, however, is more like a big department store than a mall. The items are arranged in categories, and you can even use a search engine to find what you're looking for. The emphasis is not on grouping the items according to seller. eBay groups items according to categories.

eBay Stores is different. You can search through categories and you can search for specific items, but you can also search according to vendors. eBay Stores is literally a huge mall with over 140,000 stores. It must be considered the largest mall on the Internet, and that in and of itself is a huge attractor. The eBay brand works to make this unique mall successful.

Nonetheless, eBay Stores are not nearly as successful as eBay itself—that is, eBay auctions. I believe eBay Stores will gradually emerge as a viable online mall, a powerful marketplace. Still, to get there, it will have evolved in a unique historical way. It will have clearly defied what seems to be a general rule on the Web—that general malls do not work.

Amazon.com

Amazon.com is itself a huge department store on the Web. It started with books but then expanded into other merchandise. And then of all things, it enabled other vendors to join it in what is analogous to a large online mall that co-exists with the Amazon department store itself. Amazon Marketplace (*http://www.amazon.com/exec/obidos/subst/misc/sell-your-stuff.html*), as it is called, has been somewhat successful. But its success is not necessarily because it is a great online mall, but rather because Amazon is a great brand. In any event, it is not so successful as eBay or eBay Stores.

Brand names aside, if you really want to understand what makes eBay and eBay Stores work, look at the fees charged. They are so low that retail businesses on eBay can operate efficiently and offer substantially lower prices than bricks-and-mortar businesses or identical or similar businesses elsewhere online. In other words, it's less expensive to do business on eBay and eBay Stores than in other major Web malls. And therein lies the secret of eBay's success and the success of all eBay's retail selling members.

Differences

Just for the sake of clarity let's explore the differences between Web malls, portals, search engines, and competitive shopping directories. Sometimes the differences are not apparent because many websites tend to be hybrids.

Web Malls Web malls are simply aggregators of diverse retail vendors which offer very little or no content to attract website visitors other than the shopping.

Portals Portals are Web information centers for specific topics. As part of the massive content they provide to website visitors, they may also offer specialized shopping.

Search Engines When search engines are used as shopping

devices, they merely search the Web for a specific product entered by a Web shopper. They usually return a list of vendors mixed in with other information sources relevant to the product. Specialized search engines such as Froogle and Yahoo Shopping eliminate all of the non-commercial resources and feature only the product for sale by different vendors. But the search engines are not aggregators of Web retailers as are Web malls.

Comparative-Shopping Directories Comparative-shopping directories in a sense are aggregators of Web retailers. Web retailers export a datafeed to become, in effect, *members* of a comparative-shopping directory. A directory provides a website visitor with a table (layout) that lists vendors compared according to price and reputation.

There are two things to note when you read the above four definitions. First, many sites are hybrids. For instance, if a portal robust with information starts to sell a lot of products, it starts to look like a Web mall. Likewise, if a Web mall starts loading on a lot of content to attract website visitors, it starts to look like a portal.

Second, you will note that for Web malls and portals there is a definite sense of place. In other words, there is a place on the Web where the mall or the portal can be found, and is always the same place (i.e., the same URL).

The search engines and the comparative-shopping directories are not the same. There is no sense of place. There isn't even any sense of sameness. You can use a set of keywords today and get one list of links to products in a search-engine return. Tomorrow you can use the same keywords and get a slightly or perhaps even radically different list. Use slightly different keywords, and you may get a completely different list.

The comparative-shopping directories are like the search engines. When you search for one product, you might get a very short list of links from a comparative-shopping directory. When you search for a similar product, you may get a much longer list. The returns expand and contract, often unpredictibly. Such results do not instill in you the idea of a place on the Web. The returns from search engines and comparative-shopping directories seem to exist somewhere out in the cyber ether. (Of course, once you click a link and go to a specific vendor to buy something, presumably you will get a sense of place.)

Although eBay Stores seems clearly a Web mall and indeed one that's likely to be ultimately quite successful, eBay auctions seem to be a hybrid between a Web mall and a search engine.

Affitliate Programs

Affiliates are websites that allow you to sell your products on their websites. You provide a link from an affiliate website to your website, or you provide a special section (group of webpages) to be added to the affiliate's website. You need to have software that keeps track of the business that comes in from each affiliate so that you can pay each its sales commissions.

Although you can buy software or software services that will automate affiliate administration for you, you still have to make the initial arrangements yourself. Yes, it's true that some affiliate software enables potential affiliates to sign up online to be affiliates and then integrates them into the tracking system. But you're going to get your most productive affiliates by recruiting them and then keeping them happy.

For many products, affiliate marketing works well. For many years it was an inviting means of marketing on the Web. Today with the advent of eBay, eBay Stores, Google, and Froogle, and their capture of a large market share in ecommerce, affiliate programs are not as important to most online retailers as they once were.

For more information on affiliate programs try Affiliate Guide (*http://www.affiliateguide.com*) or LinkShare (*http://www.linkshare.com*).

That will get you started. Affiliate software is commonly available. For instance, a third-party makes an affiliate plug-in program for Miva Merchant, thus converting that very capable ecommerce program into an affiliate manager.

Cost-Effectiveness Review

The automation of affiliate maketing with software makes it cost-effective. Unfortunately, each affiliate relationship is a business relationship that must be initiated and nurtured via personal contact. This takes a lot of time and may no longer be cost-effective.

Sales Management

This is basic economics. In the first place, you don't want to sell in a market niche where there is a glut of identical or similar products. Prices—and profits—will be low, and the competition will be dibilating for you. So ideally, as explained in *eBay Business the Smart Way* Second Edition, you will want to sell in a niche that's big enough to be profitable but small enough to discourage competion.

That doesn't mean that you won't be able to achieve a high volume of sales. If you have little competition, a high volume of sales might become the cornerstone of of your retailing effort. The question becomes, How do I achieve a high volume of sales without anyone knowing about it?

You might ask, What difference does it make if anyone knows about it? Well first, if potential buyers perceive that there's a lot of inventory up for auction, they won't be willing to pay as high a price as they would if they perceived that few items were available. Indeed, they may wait to buy until the price goes down just because there are lots of auctions and the perception is that some auctions may not receive bids. The more you sell openly in public, the lower the price will be. Second, a huge number of visible sales may attract competitors who think a large market exists. Neither of these situations is desirable.

So, the goal becomes to sell as much as possible but create the perception that the product is in limited supply. The first step in this strategy is to refrain from using a Dutch auction. Clearly Dutch auctions will draw attention to the fact that you have a large supply of the product on hand.

The second step is to use a combination of normal auctions and auctions with a Buy-It-Now fixed price. You can also use the second-chance offer effectively.

Classic Case

The classic case of effective sales management took place offline in the last decade and was engineered by Ty, Inc., with its marketing of Beanie Babies. Each "model" of Beanie Baby was marketed in a unique production quantity and later "retired." This created a different supply and demand ratio for each model. As a result, some Beanie Babies grew to be worth $25 and some $2,500 on the secondary market. But Ty retailers sold most all of them originally between $5 and $15. Ty retailers sold millions and millions not because Beanie Babies were better than any other stuffed animal-like toy, but because Ty managed the sales in such a way as to make Beanie Babies a collector's item. The resulting collector frenzy lasted for several years and probably would have lasted longer except that a flood of counterfeit Beanie Babies from China disrupted Ty's carefully orchestrated sales.

Combination Auctions

How do you keep your sales high without the illusion of too much inventory being on the market? You use fixed-price (Buy-It-Now) auctions. Unlike a normal auction, which last at least a few days, a fixed-price purchase is instant—as soon as a buyer materializes. And you can replace it instantly with another fixed-price auction. Consequently, without the illusion of flooding the market with auctions, you can generate high sales. The trick is to keep the right balance of normal auctions and fixed-price auctions simultaneously to keep sales high and visibility low.

Second-Chance Offers

eBay instituted the second-chance offer program to protect sellers against nonpaying buyers. If your highest bidder doesn't complete the transaction, you can offer the item to the runner-up bidder. In fact, eBay has extended the program to cover multiple runner-up bidders. And you pay no listing fees to take advantage of these extra sales. In other words, you can sell multiple identical items from one auction without anyone except eBay being the wiser.

Management

To manage sales, you need to use the combination auctions, second-chance offers, and any other techniques you can dream up to sell in volume without creating visibility. See Chapter 5 of Scot Wingo's book *eBay Strategies* (Prentice Hall) for details on how to sell in volume without the public perceiving the volume. It pays to have a good auction mangement service that can faciliate or automate such sales schemes to save you the management work.

Even Without Visibility

Even without visibility you can still saturate the market for your product. You need to find the balance point between your supply and the demand.

Remember that sales management is appropriate for a product. It makes good sense. However, when you have several products or dozens of products, the management tasks can grow to be burdensome. Nonetheless, you need to tend the sales, and it's unlikely that you will be able to do so well without help from specialized software.

Cost-Effectiveness Review

The cost-effectiveness of this technique to a large degree depends on your use of an auction management service. If software can help you do what has to be done for sales management, this technique can prove worthwhile. If you have to tend it all yourself, it will take a lot of time. Regardless, sales management is a necessary part of marketing.

Categories

As mentioned in Chapter 5, using the proper keywords is crucial to writing good titles for eBay auction ads. Not all potential eBay buyers, however, use keywords and the eBay search engine. Some work their way down through the category tree to find items. This makes placing your items in the right categories quite important and must be considered a prime marketing tactic. What's the right category? That's for you to find out.

The best way to do so is simply to look for similar or identical items. Where you find them is where your item belongs. This is simple research, but it takes time, particularly when you start selling multiple new items from time to time.

Sometimes you will find multiple places appropriate for an item. Then you need to decide which place in the category tree to use or whether to put your item in two or three places (categories).

This seems like a small elementary topic to discuss in an advanced eBay marketing book. Perhaps it is. But it's an important concept. And the small things add up to to have a major impact on your sales.

Cost-Effectiveness Review

You don't have a choice but to carefully put your items in their proper categories. So, cost-effectiveness isn't an issue. But, yes, being careful with your category placement is worthwhile.

Satisfaction Guarantee

Give a satisfaction guarantee. This is not a product guarantee. You guarantee that your customer will be satisfied. If he isn't for any reason, he can return the merchandise for a refund.

Does this work? You bet. The mail order business is based on satisfaction guarantees. And the mail order business has been growing every year for a long long time. Leading offline retailers also offer satisfaction guarantees. This is a great marketing strategy.

As a practical matter, you may have to provide a satisfaction guarantee even if you don't offer it. Your eBay feedback rating may depend on it. So, why not offer it to promote more sales?

Cost-Effectiveness Review

A satisfaction guarantee is going to cost you. You will get returned merchandise. You have to take that into account in your pricing strategy. But it takes the fear out of dealing with you. Prospective buyers will find your guarantee enticing. I believe it is a cost-effective marketing technique for most products.

Link Trading

It's a great idea to trade links with other websites that are relevant to your own. Why? Search engines, particularly Google, base their rankings in the search engine returns on how many websites are linked to your website. It also gives weight to the size and importance of the websites linked to your website. The more links you have and the more important the websites that are linked to you, the higher your ranking will be in the search-engine results. Naturally, your goal is to get to be the number one entry in the search-engine rankings or, at least, be someplace on the first page. The first page usually contains about 10 websites.

Moreover, there is another obvious reason why links from other websites can be important to you. Website visitors to other websites are likely to click on such links which will bring them to your website. So they have the potential of driving extra traffic to your website.

Create Your Links

When you ask another website to include a link to your website on one or more of its webpages, provide it with the link sentence and the link. The link sentence including the linking words should be constructed in such a way as to optimize being found by the search engines and getting a higher ranking in the search-engine returns.

Before you make a request to another website to trade links, take a look at that website and determine where you would like the links to your website to be. Then specify those webpages in your request. Of course, there is no certainty that the other website will grant your request, but it never hurts to ask. You also need to determine where on your website that you will put the reciprocal links. In addition, you have to determine what your policy will be for requests from other websites to have their links put on a special page in your website.

Getting Organized

Once you trade more than a few links, keeping your link trading organized presents a serious problem. Nonetheless you will want to keep a record of the links that you've traded. You will want to keep the other websites honest, just as they will want to keep you honest. Thus, periodically you will need to check up to see whether your links are still viable on their websites. Likewise, they will want to check up to see that their links on your website are still viable.

Hence, you need to develop a database to keep track of your link-trading relationships. However, there is an easier way. You can find link-trading software that will go a long ways towards automating the whole process for you. (Try Arelis at *http://axandra.com*.) Such software starts by finding other relevant websites on the Web with which you have a potential for establishing mutually beneficial reciprocal links. It also sends out and keeps track of email request letters. After such software gets you off to a good start in link trading, it also maintains your link-trading relationships.

Unfortunately the link-trading software does not necessarily eliminate work that must be done to set up and operate a link-trading program. It will take effort on your behalf or on the behalf of one of your employees. Still, the software will make your work more efficient and shorter in duration than if you tried to do this without software support.

Link-Trading Circles

Don't join a link-trading circle where everyone in the group trades links with every other member of the group. Some of the search engines, particularly Google, can detect such an arrangement. When it does detect such an arrangement, you may go to the bottom of the search-engine rankings or even disappear altogether. So, you need to establish your link trades individually with a one-on-one relationship.

A good policy to follow is to communicate with your link-trading partners periodically. One way to do this is to provide your link-trading partners with statistics regarding the number of click-throughs that they get from your website. See Chapter 26 regarding analytics for more information on doing this. Your periodic communication will remind them that you are still partners, and they are a lot less likely to inadvertently or purposely erase your links on their websites. In addition, it's a friendly gesture to keep the door open for future discussions about how you might cooperate. Indeed, occasionally you will want to review your partnerships with these other websites to determine what other mutually beneficial relationships you can create.

Banner Trading

You can do the same thing with banners that you do with links. That is, you can trade them. After all, banners are nothing but graphics with a link in them.

A good way to get off to a good start with a new website is go on a link-trading campaign, and attempt to establish as many reciprocal links as possible. You don't have to do it that way, however; you can do it piece-meal. You can find a few trades every week and someday that effort will add up to a lot of reciprocal-link trades. But the point is to start it now.

The Guru's Viewpoint

The search engine guru that I consult with believes that reciprocal links don't work well for getting found by the search engines. One-way links work much better according to him. In other words, if you can arrange links from another website to your website without reciprocation, the search engines will give you a boost. How do you accomplish this? You work hard at it. It helps to have a great website.

Cost-Effectiveness Review

This is a technique to increase your website traffic that requires only your time and a little bit of software. It's not something you have to do all at once, and it needn't take a huge front-end effort. It's something you can do a little bit at a time, and that will eventually build into something big. This is a valuable technique that you do not want to overlook.

If you are not optimizing your website for the search engines, however, link trading is less valuable. It may not be cost-effective purely as a means of building traffic via links from other websites.

A Contest

Run a contest. Make it fun. The bigger the prize, the more interest you'll generate with a contest. Contests have certainly worked well for retailers from time immemorial. It's no different on the Web. This is the kind of marketing project that will take some of your time and energy, but if you can generate enough excitement with a contest, it may be worthwhile.

Cost-Effectiveness Review

It's difficult to make a statement about the cost-effectiveness of a contest. It depends on the amount of time and energy you put into it and the cost of the prize. Beyond that, however, it depends on the advertising it takes to make it an effective sales campaign. Realistically, it must be considered a variant of advertising—an advertising campaign with a twist.

A Sale

Can you hold a sale online? Sure, why not? All you need is a graphic or a collection of graphics explaining your sale. For instance, one graphic might say, "Sale!". Another might say, "20% Off". You put those two graphics in a catalog webpage, and you have put an item on sale.

A sale is something offline retailers do to move excess merchandise or to generate traffic. A clever eBay retailer shouldn't have any excess merchandise (read *eBay Business the Smart Way* Second Edition), but one can't be clever 100 percent of the time. To generate traffic, the sale must be combined with advertsing. Then it becomes a variant of advertising.

Backoffice

When you run a sale, don't forget to pay attention to your backoffice operations. You want to make sure that your checkout procedure calculates the correct prices for sale items while they are on sale. Most good ecommerce programs will include provisions for running sales easily so that sales will be convenient for you.

Marketing

Sales are probably the most important and most widely used marketing technique for all retailers. That may be true online too. You will want to experiment with sales and perhaps make them a regular feature of your eBay Store retailing. But you can even run a sale in an eBay auction. You might advertise something like, "For a limited time only, a lower reserve price." And, of course, you can claim that your Buy-It-Now price is lower for a certain period during the sale.

Sales, to be meaningful, have to convey some benefits. They should offer your merchandise at a lower price than is normal but only for a specified period of time. If you run sales consistently this way, they will generate revenue for you.

If you merely offer your merchandise at sale prices all the time, however, as some websites do, you will probably find it to be an ineffective marketing technique. I get the impression from a website that runs a perpetual sale that it isn't maintained properly. The sale, in effect, becomes stale, and prospective customers will not trust the website to be current. If prospective customers sense that the website is not current, they will be reluctant to make a purchase at any price.

Excitement

In my view, the best reason to run a sale on the Web is for a special reason: to create a change. Websites and webpages tend to be static. A sale causes a little excitement. Just by adding two or three sale graphics and lowering prices for a period, you change a webpage. Just like a perpetual sale is perceived as stale, a sale with a certain begining and end is perceived as dynamic merchandising. It's a great way to bring a dynamic quality to a seemingly static medium. Just make sure you end it at the advertised end.

Cost-Effectiveness Review

A sale is easy and inexpensive to run, particularly if your auction management service enables sales. A sale does cost you lost revenue. A sale that offers 20 percent off your normal price will generate 20 percent less revenue. A sale run to generate traffic requires advertsing. Thus, cost-effectivenss depends on a number of factors. But it seems that a sale will not be at the top of your list of cost-effective marketing techniques.

It doesn't matter. I believe you need to run sales just to create excitment at your eBay Store or independent website. It's the kind of excitement that brings people back and builds your brand over the long term, but it's sometimes difficult to measure. It's an essential part of aggressive marketing, and to be as successful as you can be as an eBay retail business, you need to market aggressively.

Points

Points are a means to reward existing customers so that they will buy in the first place and have an incentive to return to purchase more in the future. Running a points system would be an administrative nightmare without using the proper point-system software. Consequently, you will need a vendor to provide a point system to you.

There is also such a thing as a point system on a broader scale; that is, a point system where people can use their points to buy merchandise from other retailers too. Some of the point-system vendors have set up their systems that way and are trying to establish a brand. The better they can brand their point system, the more desirable the points will become. The more desirable the points are, the better the point system will help sell your merchandise. Thus, if you get involved in such a point system, it pays to choose a vendor that's well branded.

eBay offers such a point system now called Anything Points. Read about the program at *http://anythingpoints.ebay.com/offer.html*. It's there for your use as a seller. All you have to do is take advantage of it. eBay is promoting this point system, and if you're going to give points, eBay points should certainly be one of the systems that you consider.

I am a little skeptical of points. I don't think they work as well as some of the other techniques discussed in this chapter. However, as I have said before, they may work very well for some products and not very well for others. So, it's up to you to experiment to see whether they work for your retail business. Fortunately, the eBay points system makes it very easy for you to try out this marketing technique. But don't overlook other vendors that may offer point systems more suited to your products.

Cost-Effectiveness Review

It's easy to offer points in any point system. For example, it's easy to offer Anything Points. But it costs you. eBay's Anything Points are worth 1 cent each. You can offer 1 to 10 points per dollar of sales price. That's a 1 to 10 percent discount, in effect. So, that's your cost. Are points worth a 1 to 10 percent discount? That is, will they generate enough extra sales to justify the cost? Like I said, I'm skeptical. But experiment to determine whether points will work for your eBay retail business.

Surveys

HTML includes a provision for making input into a webpage, whether it be actual text or just making an election in a check box. This enables you to run a survey in a webpage. Does a survey sell merchandise? No. But a survey can gather useful information from your prospective buyers or your actual customers. Once you gather that information, you can use it in planning your marketing projects.

People are asked to fill out surveys all the time, much more so than in prior years, and most are reluctant to waste their time to do so. Consequently, you have to give people an incentive to complete your survey. That incentive can be anything from a free gift to a 25 percent discount on the next purchase.

You will definitely want to include survey-like questions when you get a new customer in order to gather as much information as possible about that customer. You can't go overboard, or you will turn people off. Nonetheless you should be able to get something more than just a person's name, phone number and address. So, a few survey questions should be part of the sign-up procedure for every new customer.

A clever auction management service might ask a customer a few new questions each time they buy something as part of the check out procedure. Thus, the data for that customer will accumulate.

Cost-Effectiveness Review

Like many other online techniques, this one is most cost-effective when automated. Look to your auction management service to gather information from customers. Running surveys apart from your normal transactional processes takes more of your time and is only as cost-effective as the data gathered is useful for increasing sales.

CRM

Customer relations management (CRM) is a big deal for large businesses with enterprise computer networks. CRM is the means, software, and Internet devices that enable a large business to manage customer relationships efficiently and in an organized manner. Major software companies such as Siebel, Oracle, SAP, and IBM provide the means for integrating CRM with normal business procedures. Is this available only to large companies?

The answer is yes and no. In fact, many of the auction management services include CRM techniques and processes. For instance, many manage the email communications between you and your customers. On the other hand, some of the corporate CRM systems encompass practically everything customer-related from beginning to end.

The whole point of managing customer relationships is that your existing customers are your best prospects for future sales. CRM enables you to provide your customers with a satisfying purchasing experience and after-sale relationship.

You can expect the CRM features of auction management software to grow in the future. In the meanwhile, when you choose an auction management service, you will want to evaluate the CRM features. Also, you need to stay alert for new CRM software that becomes available for small businesses. Give it a good look to see what it can do for you and your customers.

Cost-Effectiveness Review

As this type of software becomes integrated into the auction management services and otherwise becomes available to small businesses, it will be yet another example of how digital technology is equally available to small businesses as well as large, and at an affordable cost. Yes, this is cost-effective, and you will need it more and more in the future to remain competitive.

Trade Shows

Trade shows are informative and even fun. They are essential for being the most successful you can be. But they can also be inconvenient. It's too easy to tell yourself, I can't go this year but I'll go next year.

eBay Live

When innovative new marketing techniques for online commerce come along, you are most likely to see them first at a trade show. Your trade show is eBay Live, the annual eBay conference. It has been held in the following cities:

Anaheim
Orlando
New Orleans

In June 2005, the fourth will be held in San Jose, California, eBay's home town, for the eBay tenth anniversary. With over 100 eBay industry vendors, you will find a wide range of products, services, and software designed to help you operate your eBay retail business. Many of the products, services, and software are marketing devices and techniques to help you make more sales. This is the place to keep up to date on the latest marketing schemes.

Product Trade Shows

Find trade shows to attend that are relevant to your products. Attendance will keep you up to date and ahead of competitors on the latest industry developments and new products. Read *eBay Business the Smart Way* Second Edition for more details on trade shows.

Cost-Effectiveness Review

Are trade shows cost-effective? Yes. Trade shows are invaluable. As mentioned above, attending trade shows relevant to your products will keep you ahead of competitors in regard to the latest merchandise. eBay Live will help you keep your eBay marketing at its most cost-effective.

eBay's Hidden Market

You can sell as much stuff off eBay as you can on eBay just by being aware of the eBay hidden market. You don't have to violate any eBay rules. The fact is that the items you auction on eBay are, in effect, advertisements for identical or similar goods that you have in inventory but are not currently up for auction on eBay. What you say in your auction ads can encourage or discourage off-eBay transactions.

For instance, suppose you're selling a set of 8 wine glasses on eBay. Someone needs 72. What does he do to get 72 from you?

Even your eBay customers are potential buyers in the hidden market. Suppose, you sell a set of 8 steak knives on eBay. The person decides to give identical sets as Christmas presents. She needs 6 more sets. What does she do to get 6 more sets from you?

eBay Business the Smart Way Second Edition covers the hidden market in more detail and what you can do to take advantage of it.

Cost-Effectiveness Review

The hidden market is cost-effective, because it costs little and has the potential for substantial sales. The risk is that if you don't closely observe eBay rules, you may find yourself bounced off eBay. But sales in the hidden market can be sought without breaking eBay rules.

Craig's List

I've been saying since my first eBay book in 1999 that eBay hasn't figured out how to do local auctions (local marketplaces) yet. eBay created a local auction mechanism and featured it on the eBay website for a long period and then buried it. It still exists waiting for a day in the future to be revived.

In the meanwhile, Craig's List (*http://craigslist.com*) has figured out a workable formula for a successful local marketplace. It started in the San Francisco Bay Area in 1995 and expanded to several other cities including New York. Where Craig's List has matured, it is a very effective local marketplace. Recently it expanded to almost 60 cities including three in Canada, three in the UK, one in Ireland, and two in Australia. Although most of these Craig's List marketplaces are not mature yet, they are on the way.

eBay Motors the Smart Way and *eBay Business the Smart Way* Second Edition each covered Craig's List briefly. Then what do you suppose happened? eBay bought a 25 percent interest in Craig's List (from a private investor) in August 2004. Could it be that Craig's List will be an eBay family member someday? Who knows?

What's important for you to know is that Craig's List, where it's avaiable, is a viable marketplace opportunity for you. It is particularly appropriate for large or heavy items that cannot be shipped via the Postal Service, UPS, FedEx, or DHL.

There's a couple of things to keep in mind. First, Craig's List is not designed for commercial use. It's designed for consumer-sellers. There is no efficient means of listing multiple items (i.e., no off-the-shelf software, no datafeed). Second, you can list an item only in one city. Third, if a horde of retailers started flooding Craig's List with bulk listings, it probably wouldn't work as well as it does now. Nonetheless, it's a great marketplace for things like treadmills, appliances, and furniture, which must be shipped by truck to other cities. Local delivery for such items, though, is easy. The buyer just borrows a friend's pickup truck or van and drives across town to pick up the item.

As an online marketing technique, Craig's List has its limitations. But for the appropriate merchandise, you may find it a valuable and cost-effective means of selling products in many of America's largest cities.

Cost-Effectiveness Review

Craig's List doesn't charge for item listings. They're free. Nonetheless, the listings are not conducive to automation. You may have to spend more time putting something on Craig's List than you do for other online-retail systems. Such a loss of time reduces the cost-effectiveness of Craig's List, but it can be cost-effective nonetheless for certain items.

Cost-Effectiveness Review Procedures

There are many more online-marketing techniques than this book has covered, although the book includes the major ones applicable to eBay businesses. When presented with new marketing opportunities, you need to keep some procedures in mind. Here are some guidelines for evaluating marketing schemes:

1. Never purchase or contract to set up a marketing scheme on impulse. Always take at least a few days to carefully evaluate the offering.

2. Carefully evaluate how much of your time, effort, and money will be required to set up and run the marketing scheme effectively.

3. Once you determine how much of your time or an employee's time it will take to make the marketing work, decide whether it's worth it.

4. Compare resources. Time and money are your two primary resources. Any decision to inaugurate a new marketing scheme should not only carefully evaluate each but then compare. For instance, a proposed marketing scheme may cost nothing. But if it takes a lot of your time, it may be unworkable. Likewise, a marketing project may not take any of your time. There are plenty of vendors who will do it all for you. But if the price is outrageous, it may not be financially feasible for you to put the plan into effect.

5. Ask for referrals. Then use the referrals. Talk with other eBay retail businesses—preferably ones similar to your eBay business—about the effectiveness and cost-effectiveness of the scheme. This can often be an eye-opener.

6. Go back to #2 and re-read "set up and run" and ponder its significance. It's all too easy to evaluate what it takes to get some-

thing set up and ignore what it takes to run it. Often the maintenance (the ongoing operation) is the biggest part of the job. If you have more schemes than you can maintain effectively, that in itself can derail your marketing effort.

7. Be judicious. Don't try to run a contest, run a sale, offer points, and take a survey all at the same time on the same website. You will either confuse your potential buyers and existing customers, or you will give them a case of marketing fatigue. Or both. Try marketing techniques one at a time, and evaluate each carefully to see how effective it is.

8. Measure. All the techniques discussed in this chapter and, indeed, all the techniques discussed in the entire book boil down to one final step. Measurement. If you can't measure how effective a marketing scheme is, you will be speculating. You might as well play the commodities market. Consequently Chapter 26, the last chapter in this book, discusses measuring your marketing efforts.

The considerations above will add some realism to each scheme that comes your way. And realism creates a solid basis for making good business decisions.

25

Building Your Brand

Branding is an advertising and promoting pursuit. As such, it occupies some of the most creative professionals in business. Each branding guru has his or her own idea about the definition of branding. Consequently, branding is an activity that seems to have no widely accepted standard definition. But the thread that seems to be common to most definitions is that branding is everything you do in your relationships with your customers and prospective buyers. That means that every contact you have with a customer or prospective buyer is a branding opportunity. Such an opportunity can result in success or failure. That is, the experience that the customer or prospective buyer has with your business will motivate him or her to be loyal, indifferent, or disgruntled. How well you handle such opportunities determines how successful you will be in making your brand work.

What Will You Brand?

Branding takes resources and effort. You don't have the time and resources to brand your individual items (assuming they're unbranded), unless you have just a few products that you plan to sell forever. Consequently, most eBay businesses will attempt to brand their business, not their products. This chapter focuses on branding your business and specifically your business name.

How Do You Brand?

What you do to promote your business is branding. If you can promote your business well enough to gain recognition from your customers, you will be well on your way to establishing a brand. Here are some practical ideas for building your brand:

1. Know the market.

2. Keep your products and your sales effort up to date.

3. Provide outstanding value.

4. Use customer service to generate customer loyalty.

5. Pursue excellence.

6. Build brand recognition through advertising (online and offline), public relations, and marketing.

7. Leverage your marketing via eBay.

eBay is committed to helping eBay businesses build their brands and gives them many opportunities to do so on eBay.

Start with a Name

You start your branding when you pick a name. Pick a simple name. Would you buy a laundry bleach named *Mild Sodium Hypochloride Solution for Laundering* from the Sodium Hypochloride Bottling and Processing Corporation? Would you buy *Clorox*? Keep it simple.

The point is to enable customers to recognize it; that is, remember it when they see it. So, keep it simple and keep it understandable. If your brand is *Elechron*, who's going to recognize it? If it's *ElegantClocks*, it's at least understandable.

The name should address the niche you are selling into. For example, if you're selling nice clocks, a name like *ElegantClocks* gets right to the point. A name like *Sathutral Merchandise Company* doesn't say anything about what you're selling.

Keep the name easy to spell and pronounce too. No one is going to have trouble with *ElegantClocks*. But how do you spell or pronounce *Elechron* or *Sathutral*?

If you don't sell in a niche but instead sell anything you can get at wholesale, use a name that reflects that type of business. How about *All Goods Emporium*?

Uniform Name

Use your business name uniformly throughout all your business operations. Your name should be the same for your:

- Assumed name or legal name
- Trademark
- Logo
- Internet domain name
- Website
- Email address

- Email signature
- Direct email
- eBay ID
- eBay Store name
- eBay Store Web address
- AOL ID, MSN ID, and Yahoo ID
- Froogle, Yahoo, and other datafeed marketplaces
- Telephone directory
- eBay auction ads and Store ads
- Froogle, Yahoo, and other datafeed ads
- Banner advertising
- Keyword advertising
- Letterhead
- Business cards
- Mailing labels
- Invoices, receipts, and packing slips
- Newsletter
- Legal and quasi-legal documents
- Everything else

Don't dilute your brand by operating under more than one business name. And do put your name (brand) on everything. Everything!

Don't Use "eBay" in Your Name

Don't use "eBay" in the name of your business. If you do, sooner or later you'll hear from eBay's lawyers. "eBay" is a protected trademark.

But do use eBay in a subtitle on your stationery, cards, advertisements, and the like. Example: *ElegantClocks* – Selling Clocks on eBay Since 2002.

Do You Need a Logo?

It takes more time and resources to make a logo stick, unless the logo includes your business name. Instead, just use your business name consistently. If you insist on having a logo, just use a specific typeface to make a typeface logo.

Remember that *Coca-Cola* is just a fancy typeface logo. You can easily make a typeface logo too.

You use a specific typeface in an image editor (i.e., the same one you use for editing photographs) to create a typeface logo. You can make the typeface any color with any color background (or a transparent background) and give your name a drop-shadow or some other simple enhancement.

ElegantClocks

If you're looking for something a little unusual, try the T.26 Digital Type Foundry (*http://www.t26.com*). They sell new typefaces created by independent typeface artists, and each typeface appears only once in the T.26 periodic catalog.

Keep It Readable

Hey! Some of the typefaces available now are very cool but difficult to read. For branding, you need a typeface that's not just readable but *easy to read*.

Logo

If you get talked into using a graphic logo by some enterprising digital artist who proposes to create one for you, keep the following in mind:

1. Do include your business name in the graphic logo in an easily readable form. A logo that doesn't include your business name will be much more difficult to establish as a brand.

2. Have the logo created as a vector graphic. You will be able to make it larger or smaller without any loss of quality and employ it for a wide variety of uses. Make sure it looks good small as well as large.

3. Also, make sure it looks good in black & white as well as color. Then you can use it for business documents as well as on the Web.

4. Consider registering it as a trademark.

I have nothing against logos. They're great. For a small business, however, the most efficient logo is one that includes your business name. That's why a typeface logo makes sense. It is your name. And you can create it yourself, although an artist is likely to do a better job than you or me of choosing an appropriate typeface for an attractive typeface logo.

Domain Names

For your website, you need a domain name. One way to look at the domain-name situation today is that the pickings are slim. All the straightforward one-word names are gone, owned by someone else.

They have value because they're easy to remember, and people actually use them to find things. For instance, if you sold clocks and put up a website at *clocks.com*, your customers would be able to remember your website address easily. A certain number of people looking for clocks will just type in "clocks.com" to see if they can find some, and they would find your website.

Still, millions of two-word combinations are still available. Many might be suitable for your website and your business. For instance, "elegantclocks.com" might be available and might fit your clock business. Or, how about "jonesclocks.com" if your name is Jones?

Your Domain Name

If you are starting from scratch, make your business name and your website address the same. It will be easier to build your brand, and it will be more convenient for your customers to find you:

> Elegant Clocks (*elegantclocks.com*)
>
> ElegantClocks (*elegantclocks.com*)
>
> Jones Clocks (*jonesclocks.com*)
>
> JonesClocks (*jonesclocks.com*)

Avoid extensions such as *.net*, *.org*, *.biz*, and the like. The good one-word names are taken for those extensions too, and the offbeat extensions will make it confusing for your customers to use your Web address. Stick with *.com*.

Go to the Whois search at *http://www.netsol.com* to find out if a name you have chosen is available. If not, choose another. You can register a domain name for as little as $9 per year at a domain-name registrar (e.g., *http://godaddy.com*). As soon as you make your choice, register the name immediately. Someone else could make the same choice at any time and register the name before you.

Keep in mind that your email address will be the same as your website.

suzanne@elegantclocks.com

suzanne@jonesclocks.com

or

admin@jonesclocks.com

sales@jonesclocks.com

staff@jonesclocks.com

Domain names are not case sensitive; that is, the characters can be uppercase or lowercase or any combination. Thus, you can publish the Web addresses mentioned as:

ElegantClocks.com

JonesClocks.com

Suzanne@ElegantClocks.com

Sales@JonesClocks.com

Names are important. Take some time to read about domain names in an Internet book and familiarize yourself with how they work.

eBay ID

Make your eBay ID the same as your domain name to help build your brand. The easier you can make things for your customers, the better. This will require your coordinating an eBay ID that's available with a domain name that's available.

If you're dead set on getting a one-word name that suits your business, that name may be available for sale. Look up the owner in Whois, and try to negotiate a purchase. The value of domain names seems to go up and down with NASDAQ (the virtual stock market). When NASDAQ is low, you may be able to purchase the domain name you want inexpensively.

Your eBay Store Domain

Your eBay Store Web address is unique. It uses hyphens between words to make sense. For instance, your business ElegantClocks will have the eBay Store URL of

http://stores.ebay.com/Elegant-Clocks

This Web address belongs to you just as if you had purchased a domain name. So long as you and eBay remain on good terms, you will be able to use this URL indefinitely.

This URL is a good one. The eBay part is not too difficult to remember, although it's more complex than it should be. If you use your eBay Store as the gateway to your multi-domain website, your eBay Store URL will suffice.

About Me

Your eBay About Me Web address is unique too. For instance, your business ElegantClocks will have an eBay About Me URL that matches your eBay ID.

http://members.ebay.com/ws2/eBayISAPI.dll?ViewUserPage&userid=elegantclocks

This is not exactly an easy URL to remember, and eBay ought to remedy this. If you use About Me as the gateway to your multi-domain website, this URL is something of a handicap.

Domain Prefixes

You can add a prefix to a domain name, and it's like getting a completely new domain name. For instance, if you have the domain name *clocks.com*, you can use

alarm.clocks.com

grandfather.clocks.com

sundial.clocks.com

and the like. (Only the owner of the root domain name can arrange this.) You simply put a period in front of the domain name and add whatever you want to. The prefixed domain name acts just like any other domain name. It will cost you an extra monthly fee for each additional name that you create this way with most host ISPs, but it might be worth it if you have a use for it. Unfortunately, you will have to educate your customers to put in that extra period.

Naming Case Study

I needed to build a website that supported eBay retailers so as to promote my six books about eBay. I didn't want to brand it *The Smart Way*, like the books, because I wanted it to be about more than just the books. Still, the website needed to be eBay-centric rather than about something generic such as "ecommerce." But I couldn't use the eBay name, because it's a trademark. Also, the name to be picked would be central to the branding effort. It had to be short, make sense, and relate to eBay.

It's tough enough to pick a name. It's even tougher to pick one for which you can still register the domain. Many domain names have been registered by people who just want to sell them to you.

I brainstormed for hours and checked the Whois database to determine if the names I dreamed up were unregistered. It is staggering how many names have been registered by someone else. The best I could do was *sellerssite.com*, not the most inspiring brand in recent memory.

The nice thing about getting a brainstorm started is that it doesn't necessarily end when you go to do something else like your daily chores. Sure enough, it came to me when I was out and about town running some errand. I thought of a name and looked it up on Whois as soon as I got home. It was available, and I registered it. It is:

Bayside Business, *baysidebusiness.com*

It's true. This is not the greatest brand ever dreamed up. After all, I'm just writing a chapter on branding, not a book. But it's not bad. As I build this website up over the next few years, the brand will pull its weight and more.

But just a name doesn't mean much. Amazon.com proved that. It's what you do with the name that counts. So, it will be up to me over the next few years to build a website that's valuable to eBay retailers and a brand that will remind eBay retailers to come back and visit again—and to buy books.

What does this example prove? If I found a decent name in a few hours of brainstorming alone, you can do it too. And if you find the going slow, enlist some friends and relatives for a brain-storming session or two. There are still plenty of two-word domains left unregistered.

How Else Can You Build a Brand?

What else can you do to establish your brand? You certainly can't do as much as national companies, which build national brands with millions of dollars in advertising and promotion. But you can just use it; that is, use your name in everything you do as listed earlier in the chapter.

You probably can't get your eBay customers to remember your brand in most cases. But if you can get your customers to recognize your brand when they see it, you've done about as much as you can do.

We are all bombarded with thousands of brands every week. Due to your modest resources to promote your brand as a small business, your brand probably won't stand out in the deluge. In other words, past customers probably won't remember to look for your brand when they need an item that you sell. However, when past customers return to buy similar items at a later date, you want them at least to remember your brand when they see it as they go through the list of eBay items. That is, you want them to recognize it.

Then too, if you're selling items that people buy repeatedly, your customers will come back to you on eBay regularly just as they will anywhere else. They will look for your brand. That makes developing a good brand an important part of your business effort.

Not all retail sales get repeat business within a reasonable time (e.g., digital cameras), but many do get repeat business regularly (e.g., photofinishing). For instance, people may buy digital cameras every two to five years. But the same people may have their digital photographs printed by a digital photofinisher on an average of once a month. If you sell digital cameras on eBay, a strong brand may not be important to success. If you provide a photofinishing service via eBay, however, you will need a strong brand for repeat business. (Digital photofinishing is a service that enables customers to upload their digital photograph files, which the digital photofinisher then prints and delivers via snailmail.)

Ensure Continuous Visibility

You have to have continuous visibility to have a brand. If you go to buy soft drinks in a supermarket and Coke isn't on the shelves, the Coke brand is seriously diminished. For your eBay business, you need to have plenty of auctions going all the time. You have to have high visibility on eBay. If you're not there, bidders can't recognize you.

Cross-Sell

Use the eBay Stores Cross-Promotion (see Chapter 19) or other similar devices provided by auction management services to build your brand and your sales. These are excellent techniques and are readily available. Cross-promotion works best when the items are related. If the items are not related, cross-selling is not likely to work well. For instance, when you're selling leatherworking products, cross-selling to stereo speakers isn't going to be very productive. But cross-selling to leather dyes will probably increase overall sales. Read more on cross-selling in Chapter 19.

Advertise

Advertising is the traditional means of building a brand. You can't afford the advertising dollars (millions) it takes to build a brand off the Web. On the Web, the primary way to advertise is to put banners on other websites directing potential customers to your website. This is expensive too. The only way to find out if it's cost-effective is to try it. But without your own website (or eBay Store) to which to direct potential customers, banner advertising doesn't make much sense. Read more about advertising in Chapter 20.

Provide Great Customer Service

And the winning brand builder is... Our old friend customer service! This is the best way to build your brand. This is where your focus needs to be. Without good customer service, you can't build a brand on eBay—or anywhere else. With good customer service you can build a brand over an extended period. It takes a while, but it boosts sales. Read Chapter 3 for more on customer service.

Don't confuse good sales with building a brand. A brand is about plenty of repeat sales and referrals. It is your customers coming back again and again and telling their friends and relatives about you. Good customer service is a major component of effective branding.

The Name Isn't Everything

Remember that this chapter started with a general definition of the branding concept. Then the chapter went immediately into managing a business name as your brand. But the name alone doesn't mean much. The process of branding is giving the name meaning—good meaning—through how you interact with your customers. Without using some of the core elements of good marketing to generate customer good will, your brand won't come to mean anything. In fact, without good customer service, your brand could become a liability instead of an asset.

Accordingly, to understand branding, you have to think beyond a name. Branding is everything you do in your relationships with customers. A great brand is a symbol of something else. And it's that something else that is the most important aspect of branding.

Aesthetics

As we all know, aesthetics are important for branding. In other words, your logo and marketing materials should be attractive and professional looking. Spend some money to have them professionally done. Try eLance, which you can find under the Professional Services link on the eBay home page. That's a good place to find freelancers who can do advertising, marketing, and graphics projects for you inexpensively.

Don't forget your auction ads, eBay Store, About Me, independent website, and HTML email. They should have attractive asethetics too and be graphically related by a consistant visual theme. Although the auction management services provide attractive templates—and eBay does too—having your own unique integrated designs can make your brand shine.

More on Branding

If all else fails, read the manual. That is, read a book on branding. Branding is a hot topic in business today as well as a hot topic in online business. There are many current books on branding. Try:

Brain Tattoos, Karen Post (The Branding Diva), AMACOM, 2004.

Did you notice that Ms. Post has branded herself?

The Branding Diva

She offers a "Tool Kit" for the self-employed (a checklist of branding) as well as many other aids for doing specific branding tasks.

And then there is Stan Slap who spoke at eBay Live in New Orleans. He claims to be writing a book. But you don't have to wait for it. Go to his website *http://www.slapworld.com* and ask for the free article delivered in a PDF. The title of the article is: *Fix the Future*. His topic at eBay Live: *Do Something About Your Brand Before It Does Something About You*. And what is this presentation all about? A strong thread of customer service runs through it.

Cost-Effectiveness Review

Branding is an ongoing campaign that doesn't end. You do it by using other marketing techniques effectively, such as customer service and advertising. From one point of view, it doesn't make sense to talk about branding separately from the marketing techniques you use to build your brand. From another point of view, however, you need to spend some time managing your brand, such as doing the following:

1. Ensuring consistent use of your brand

2. Aggressively using your brand for a variety of marketing and sales opportunities

3. Protecting your brand from infringement

4. Creating new marketing activities that specifically enhance your brand

5. Measuring the effectiveness of your brand

It is brand management that you need to evaluate for cost-effectiveness. Indeed, brand management is a necessary job without which the impact of your branding effort may be squandered. Brand management leverages the power of all your marketing activities and thus must be considered cost-effective and worthwhile.

26

Analytics

Well, we now have a stable full of marketing techniques. Let the horses run. The problem is that these horses don't even run on the same track. I've given my estimates of cost-effectiveness. But they're just that, estimates and opinions. There are many different types of products in the over 22 million items listed on eBay each week. The sales of your individual items will respond differently to each of the sales and marketing techniques covered. How can we tell which techniques are really effective for a product?

The answer is experiment and measure. This book will help you with your experiments and to develop a notion of the priority with which you need to conduct your experiments for each product. This chapter will help you measure the results.

Web Servers

Web servers are amazing programs. As you know, they serve up webpages speedily and efficiently to anybody who visits a website. What you may not know is they also keep detailed records. These records are actually detailed logs of the traffic that takes place on the Web server. If you went through these logs, you could find out valuable information about who visits your site and where such visitors are coming from.

Doing so, however, would be very tedious and would not be a good use of your time. Fortunately, there are programs that go through such logs for you and extract valuable information. The best place for you to find such programs is to do a search on Google and see what's available. WebTrends (*http://www.netiq.com/webtrends/default.asp*) is a good example.

You will find that there are many Web-traffic-analysis programs available that will analyze your website traffic for you. Some of them are programs that you run on your own PC, and some are programs that run separately on a server somewhere and provide the analytic services for you without using your computer. These programs and services all have a common characteristic. They cost money. Nonetheless, once you've compared these services and desktop programs and understand the kind of analytic data they can provide, you are ready to take a look at what your host ISP provides.

The host ISP for your website will usually provide some type of analytic package for you as part of its basic service. You will want to take a good look at this free analytic software service in order to determine whether it's robust enough for your purposes. If it is, there's no reason to spend money on another service. Just use the one that's available to you. If it's not a robust service and you need more, then you will have to think about either changing host ISPs or paying fees for a separate Web-analytic service.

Considerations

One of the considerations is, Where will you use this analytic service? If you will use it at your own website—presumably integrated into a multi-URL website—you can proceed as outlined in the preceding paragraphs. If you do not operate a multi-URL website as suggested in Chapter 15, then to keep tabs on your eBay Store you will have to figure out a way to analyze your Web traffic at your eBay Store. Since a website-traffic-analysis program cannot access eBay's logs, you have a serious problem in determining what traffic analysis you will be able to use. In other words, it's pretty much up to eBay and what eBay provides that will determine what kind of traffic analysis you will get.

New Services

eBay opens portions of its databases to third-party software developers for a fee. This has created many new useful services for eBay sellers already and will create more in the future. Look for new services that can give you custom eBay Stores traffic information.

What's available from eBay now?

Seller Reports Information about your eBay Store sales. Comes with the Basic Store subscription.

Traffic Reports Statistics about your eBay Store traffic. Comes with the Basic Store subscription.

Advanced Reports Advanced seller and traffic reports. Comes with the Featured or Anchored Store subscription.

When choosing what level of eBay Store you want to subscribe to, take into consideration the reports furnished for that level of participation. The additional analytic information provided may, by itself, be worth the extra cost.

What's This All About?

What do you need all of this analysis for? Well, like any good retailer anywhere, you want to know where your customers are coming from. For instance, if you had a bricks and mortar store in a suburban area of a big city, you would assume that your customers were coming from the surrounding area in the suburbs. If you did an analytic study and found that 50 percent of your customers were not coming from the suburbs but were coming from rural areas—driving in from the country—you would probably decide to do your marketing and advertising in a different way.

Classic Case

Does this seem farfetched? An early classic analysis of a suburban mall showed that the market area thought to be within a 15-mile concentric circle was as wide as 150 miles in the direction away from the city.

Likewise on the Web, you need to know where your customers are coming from. If all of your customers are coming from Froogle, that tells you something about what you need to do for marketing. If all of your customers are coming from eBay Stores, that tells you something else. If all of your customers are coming from one of the comparison shopping directories, that tells you something different. Indeed, some analytical packages can even give you a reasonably good, but not totally accurate, idea of what geographical areas your customers are coming from. There is a wealth of information in analyzing the logs in minute detail for what they will reveal about your website traffic.

For those who are concerned with privacy, what I've been discussing in this chapter is not good news. The logs are not designed for privacy. For those who are interested in marketing data, however, the capability of analytic programs to extract information from the Web-traffic logs is a real boon to retailers who want to operate their retail businesses based on fact rather than guess-work. In other words, anytime that you conduct a marketing campaign or an advertising campaign, you need to measure the results of such a campaign. Only through measurement will you be able to understand what works and what doesn't. And clearly what doesn't work is not cost-effective.

Boon or Boondoggle

Is this website-traffic analysis for real? When you think about it, it's difficult to keep track of customers in the physical world. That is, it's difficult to do it by yourself. There's plenty of expensive software and analytic services available to you to obtain and analyze data. But it's more expensive offline to get such analysis than it is online. In a sense, the Web itself has a certain amount of built-in analytic capability. And you can take advantage of that capability at a very reasonable price, or in the case of using free software at your host ISP, no price at all. Consequently, website traffic analysis is a great boon to online retailing. It enables you to tune your advertising and marketing to be more effective. Don't plan your business without it!

Other Analysis

Website traffic analysis is not the only analysis available to you. Look to your auction management services and software to see what kind of financial, sales, and traffic analysis they provide. Where there are uncovered gaps between website analysis and auction-management-service analysis, you may be able to analyze your own records to determine sources of traffic. There is clearly not one solution that fits all circumstances and all marketing and advertising programs.

Analysis is such an important part of retailing that in the future you will see more and more types of analysis become available. Keep alert to new developments, new services, and new software for retail analysis. There may be something that comes along tomorrow that can make or break your retail business.

Counters

Put visitor counters on all your eBay auctions. This will give you an idea of what your traffic is for each item. Keep records of the count and match such records to your marketing experiments.

Doing this once or twice isn't going to tell you much. Doing it routinely will build a large database of useful data for marketing analysis. If your auction management service does this, great! If not, you need to keep the results in a spreadsheet or database application. Remember, the prime message of this book is that databases are ever valuable to doing business. This is another instance where a database can help you make intelligent marketing decisions.

External Business Data and Analysis

There are two types of analysis important beyond just analyzing your own website traffic. One is an overall analysis of the market, and the other is comparative analysis to other similar businesses.

The Overall Market

There is analysis available both published in print and online —sometimes free and sometimes for a fee—that indicate how your industry is doing or even how well specific products are selling in general. When you compare your sales to either regional or national sales figures, you can often gauge how well your retail business is doing. If your sales are poor in comparison, you know that you might be doing something that's not effective. If your sales are high in comparison, you will know that your marketing and advertising campaigns are fruitful.

Sometimes you can get these types of statistics from manufacturers or distributors either in printed form, on the Web, or in conversations with manufacturers' reps. In cases where you get them verbally, write them down immediately, and put them someplace in your records where you can find them readily when you get around to analyzing your business.

What's important to understand here is that some of the auction management services provide statistical information derived from actual eBay and eBay Stores sales. These are statistics that cannot be found any other place, and it's worth a subscription to the auction management service just to get your hands on such statistics. Indeed, Andale (*http://andale.com*), for example, provides all its services in modules, and you don't even have to subscribe to anything except the analytic services that Andale provides. In other words, you can use Andale statistics without actually using Andale as your auction management service.

These services are based on eBay data and provided by Andale and others with eBay's cooperation and consent. Or, to put it more bluntly, eBay makes money by selling such information to auction management services.

These statistics are a gold mine of marketing analytic information that you would have to be crazy to go without. They present a fantastic opportunity for you to put your retail business on a rational basis. Take a good look at what's available from a variety of vendors. Then choose something that gives you the information you need to make smart decisions regarding how you allocate your resources to marketing and advertising.

AuctionBytes

The AuctionBytes website publishes weekly statistics about sales on eBay. It's a good source of general information. And it's free. Check it out at *http://auctionbytes.com*. AuctionBytes also offers a free newsletter that will keep you current on eBay news.

Comparisons

Another thing the auction management services provide is comparisons to the entire market or to other selected retailers. (The other selected retailers are not identified.) Since the other retailers are likely to be some of your competitors (even though they're unidentified), a comparison can give you a good idea of how well you're doing. Since the comparison to the other retailers is exactly the market in which you are operating, that type of comparison is often more valuable, than comparisons to general industrial statistics in your industry.

This information is accurate. It comes from eBay operations. This type of information is very unlikely to be available to you for offline retail selling. This presents another fabulous opportunity to put your retail business on a rational basis. So, you are well advised to look very carefully at what information services are available from both eBay and the auction management services. In the future, independent services that offer only information, data, and statistics will materialize to serve eBay retailers. When they do, it will be beneficial for you to take a good hard look at them to see what they offer.

Your Business Records and Analysis

Normal business records are the bottom line, in effect. When you analyze your business records, you are anlayzing the bottom line. When you match your business results to your marketing efforts and experiments, you can find out what works and what doesn't (i.e., what's profitable and what isn't). Without routinely measuring the results of your marketing efforts this way, you are merely speculating as to what is effective.

Many auction management services provide detailed analytic business reports specifically for your business based on your data. These are in addition to traffic reports, industry reports, and comparative reports. This type of "accounting" analysis is beyond the scope of this book simply because the focus here is on marketing, not operations or financial analysis. Nonetheless, it is imparitive that you use your business reports to measure your marketing. That is, you need to match your business analysis to your marketing campaigns as closely as possible.

Scot Wingo in his book about advanced eBay business practices, *eBay Strategies* (Prentice Hall, 2005), advocates the use of dashboards. His dashboards are a series of one-page business analyses that you can use to get a picture of how your eBay business is performing and also how your marketing campaigns are performing. You can find examples at *http://ebaystrategies.blogs.com*. Indeed, Mr. Wingo's reports integrate business analysis with marketing data to give you valuable information about your business. Mr. Wingo is the CEO of ChannelAdvisor (*http://channeladvisor.com*), an auction management service.

Avoid Bad Practices

Don't fall into the bad practice of paying for and accumulating market information, statistics, and data and then not using them. It takes time, effort, and attention to analyze your business. You can't do it without acquiring the requisite reports and you have to make a point of reviewing the analysis as part of your normal routine. Therefore, make it a priority that periodic analysis (e.g., monthly) is part of your normal routine.

A good way to handle this might be to hold a monthly sales meeting with your employees or your independent contractors and go over sales issues for the month. Part of that discussion can be a review of the most current marketing information, statistics, and data. Whatever you do, don't neglect the opportunity to put this fabulous information to work.

Cost-Effectiveness Review

You have at your fingertips the type of data and statistics that retailers have dreamed of for centuries. Not only do you have it at your fingertips, but it is available inexpensively. Don't pass up the opportunity to take advantage of this amazing information and put it to use to tune up your advertising and marketing campaigns and thereby tune up your retail sales. The use of information is the difference between being successful and unsuccessful or between being successful and marginally successful. Putting marketing information, statistics, and data to use is a very cost-effective way of doing business.

Epilogue

This is the end of the book. I hope that you have found plenty of information in this book that will help you generate greater sales in your eBay retail business. If you are aware of some important idea that I haven't covered in this book, I would be happy to hear from you at the following email address: jt@sinclair.com. I also operate a website, Bayside Business for eBay retail sellers, at *http://baysidebusiness.com*. You can visit that website for additional information on operating your eBay and ecommerce retail business. In addition, you can sign up for my newsletter delivered by email by going to the AMACOM website (*http://www.amacombooks.org*), the Bayside Business website, or the BookCenter website (*http://bookcenter.com*). If you are interested in expanding your sales through selling abroad, you can establish relationships with businesspeople in other countries through TradeAffiliates (*http://tradeaffiliates.com*). This is a directory that I have started in order to help people establish contact with each other from various countries in order to seek mutually beneficial trade arrangements.

I wish you the best of luck in your eBay retail business endeavors.

Appendix The Top 14 Tips for Building eBay Traffic

Top 14 tips for sellers who intend to build traffic for their eBay retail businesses.

1. Look beyond eBay and take your eBay business into the general world of ecommerce.

2. Use database techniques in your business and use datafeed marketing to expand your sales. Take advantage of Froogle's free

datafeed catalog entries.

3. Use proper placement of items in categories and appropriate use of keywords in titles to attain maximum visibility for your items.

4. Manage your eBay sales to create a high sales volume without anyone perceiving it.

5. Improve your copy writing and title writing.

6. Improve your digital photography and establish an efficient work flow.

7. Use cross-selling wherever appropriate.

8. Try advertising online, particularly keyword advertising.

9. Accept sales from buyers abroad and get set up to handle such sales safely and efficiently.

10. Be conscious about building your brand and manage your brand-building activities.

11. Apply a cost-effectiveness review to every marketing effort you consider implementing.

12. Experiment, experiment, and experiment with various marketing devices, schemes, and programs.

13. Measure your marketing efforts by tracking your sales and your profits.

14. Consider using content to build your brand and increase sales and consider building a multi-URL website that includes an independent website featuring content useful to your customers and potential buyers.

Glossary

The following words are used the following ways in this book:

Columns and Rows Columns (fields) contain pieces of data, and rows (records) contain sets of data, all in a database table.

Content Tutorials, lists, reviews, instructions, specifications, entertainment, newsletters, checklists, directories, catalogs, and other information.

Cost-Effectiveness Efficient and productive use of your time and and your money.

Datafeed An exportation of a subset of data from a database to another software application. A good example is an exportation of a subset of data from an auction management service to Froogle where the subset becomes Froogle catalog entries.

eBay Business A retailer that sells on eBay.

Independent Website A stand-alone website set up independent of eBay.

Keywords Words that express the essense of a product, service, or use of a product, and which people use to search for products and services on eBay or in search engines.

Multi-Domain Website A website that spans two or more Internet domains.

Offline Indicates a physical location (e.g., in a building). In other words, not online and not in cyberspace. "Bricks and mortar" indicates an offline establishment.

Retailer A person or company that sells products (items) to the public either as a full-time or substantial part-time business.

Third-Party You and the subject of the chapter, chapter section, or paragraph are the parties (e.g., you and eBay). A third-party is someone else. For instance, when discussing you and eBay somewhere in this book, Andale (an auction management service) is a third-party software vendor.

Vendor A person or company that sells products or services to eBay businesses. For instance, Andale is a vendor. It sells auction management services to eBay businesses. A wholesaler is a vendor.

Workflow The procedures for processing digital photographs individually or in bulk.

Index

DATE DUE		
JAN 2 3 2008		
APR 1 5 2008		
AUG 2 0 2008		
DEC 0 4 2008		
JUN 2 5 2009		